TABLE TENNIS

Steps to Success

Larry Hodges
Past Vice President
United States Table Tennis Association

in cooperation with
United States Table Tennis Association

Human Kinetics

Library of Congress Cataloging-in-Publication Data

Hodges, Larry, 1960-
    Table tennis : steps to success / Larry Hodges.
        p.   cm. -- (Steps to success activity series)
      ISBN 0-87322-403-5
      1. Table tennis. I. Title. II. Series.
    GV1005.H58   1993
    796.34'6--dc20
                                         92-37606
                                           CIP

ISBN: 0-87322-403-5

As of January 1994, the United States Table Tennis Association (USTTA) officially changed its name to USA Table Tennis (USATT).

Acquisitions Editor: Brian Holding
Developmental Editor: Judy Patterson Wright, PhD
Assistant Editors: Laura Bofinger, Valerie Hall, Moyra Knight, Julie Swadener, and Dawn Roselund
Copyeditor: Chris DeVito
Proofreader: Laurie McGee
Production Director: Ernie Noa
Typesetter and Text Layout: Kathy Boudreau-Fuoss
Text Design: Keith Blomberg
Cover Design: Jack Davis
Cover Photo: Will Zehr
Illustrations: Tim Offenstein
Printer: United Graphics

Instructional Designer for the Steps to Success Activity Series: Joan N. Vickers, EdD, University of Calgary, Calgary, Alberta, Canada

Some line drawings in "Warming Up for Success" are from *Self-Defense: Steps to Success* by Joan M. Nelson, 1991, Champaign, Illinois: Leisure Press. Copyright 1991 by Leisure Press. Adapted and reprinted by permission; from *Tennis: Steps to Success* by Jim Brown, 1989, Champaign, Illinois: Leisure Press. Copyright 1989 by Leisure Press. Reprinted by permission; and from *Weight Training: Steps to Success* by Thomas R. Baechle and Barney R. Groves, 1992, Champaign, Illinois: Leisure Press. Copyright 1992 by Leisure Press. Reprinted by permission.

Human Kinetics books are available at special discounts for bulk purchase. Special editions or book excerpts can also be created to specification. For details, contact the Special Sales Manager at Human Kinetics.

Printed in the United States of America   10

Human Kinetics
Web site: www.HumanKinetics.com

United States: Human Kinetics, P.O. Box 5076, Champaign, IL 61825-5076
800-747-4457
e-mail: humank@hkusa.com

Canada: Human Kinetics, 475 Devonshire Road, Unit 100, Windsor, ON N8Y 2L5
800-465-7301 (in Canada only)
e-mail: orders@hkcanada.com

Europe: Human Kinetics, 107 Bradford Road, Stanningley
Leeds LS28 6AT, United Kingdom
+44 (0) 113 255 5665
e-mail: hk@hkeurope.com

Australia: Human Kinetics, 57A Price Avenue, Lower Mitcham, South Australia 5062
08 8277 1555
e-mail: liaw@hkaustralia.com

New Zealand: Human Kinetics, Division of Sports Distributors NZ Ltd.
P.O. Box 300 226 Albany, North Shore City, Auckland
0064 9 448 1207
e-mail: blairc@hknewz.com

Contents

Series Preface

The Steps to Success Activity Series is a breakthrough in skill instruction through the development of complete learning progressions—the *steps to success*. These *steps* help individuals quickly perform basic skills successfully and prepare them to acquire more advanced skills readily. At each step, individuals are encouraged to learn at their own pace and to integrate their new skills into the total action of the activity.

The unique features of the Steps to Success Activity Series are the result of comprehensive development—through analyzing existing activity books, incorporating the latest research from the sport sciences and consulting with students, instructors, teacher educators, and administrators. This groundwork pointed up the need for three different types of books—for participants, instructors, and teacher educators—which we have created and together comprise the Steps to Success Activity Series.

This participant's book, *Table Tennis: Steps to Success*, is a self-paced, step-by-step guide that you can use as an instructional tool. The unique features of this participant's book include

- sequential illustrations that clearly show proper technique,
- helpful suggestions for detecting and correcting errors,
- excellent practice progressions with accompanying *Success Goals* for measuring performance, and
- checklists for rating technique.

Many of the activities in the Steps to Success Activity Series also have a comprehensive instructor's guide. However, one has not been developed for table tennis.

The series textbook, *Instructional Design for Teaching Physical Activities* (Vickers, 1990), explains the *steps to success* model, which is the basis for the Steps to Success Activity Series. Teacher educators can use the series textbook in their professional preparation classes to help future teachers and coaches learn how to design effective physical activity programs in school, recreation, or community teaching and coaching settings.

After identifying the need for various texts, we refined the *steps to success* instructional design model and developed prototypes. Once these prototypes were fine-tuned, we carefully selected authors for the activities who were not only thoroughly familiar with their sports but also had years of experience in teaching them. Each author had to be known as a gifted instructor who understands the teaching of sport so thoroughly that he or she could readily apply the *steps to success* model.

Next, all of the manuscripts were carefully developed to meet the guidelines of the *steps to success* model. Then our production team, along with outstanding artists, created a highly visual, user-friendly series of books.

The result: The Steps to Success Activity Series is the premier sports instructional series available today.

This series would not have been possible without the contributions of the following:

- Dr. Rainer Martens, Publisher,
- Dr. Joan Vickers, instructional design expert,
- the staff of Human Kinetics Publishers, and
- the *many* students, teachers, coaches, consultants, teacher educators, specialists, and administrators who shared their ideas—and dreams.

Judy Patterson Wright
Series Editor

This book is for beginning, intermediate, and advanced table tennis players. It is for those who have that deep-down desire to be a champion and those who are in it mostly for fun. Above all, this book is intended to help you make the most of your abilities, whatever your skill level. In short, this book is for you.

In these pages you'll find the many steps it takes to become a good table tennis player. Some of the steps are easy, some are hard, but all will help you in some way.

This book has allowed me to get down on paper all the playing techniques I've learned over the years. Much of the content comes from years of observing and teaching at the Olympic Training Center, and at the National Table Tennis Center with my fellow coaches Cheng Yinghua and Jack Huang. Still more has come from long discussions and even heated debates among top coaches and players I have worked with, especially Sean O'Neill and Dan Seemiller (who've won 10 U.S. men's singles titles between them), who both greatly helped in the presentation of the finer points of the game.

The techniques taught in this book are not the final word in table tennis. There are always differences of opinions among coaches in any sport, even among the best coaches in the world. This book is one correct and highly successful set of techniques, the most commonly taught ones. What makes this book unique is the way they are taught.

This book takes the reader on a table tennis journey that has been many years in the planning. In general, the progression goes from introductory principles (e.g., grip, spin, and serves), to positioning and footwork, to the shots themselves, and finally to the strategies involved. There is a logical progression of shots, starting with the simple and working up to the difficult. Each step shows how its material can be used in a real match situation. Each step integrates what is being taught with what has already been taught. Each step includes drills to practice what you've learned.

This book has many unique aspects. It stresses the importance of footwork right from the start, and it teaches both two-step and crossover footwork; it teaches the finer points of the grip, as well as covering the Seemiller grip and the Korean and Chinese penhold grips; it covers advanced serves and their techniques; it covers the return of serve, including flipping and short pushes. Each stroke description (and everything else in the book) was reviewed and approved by an editorial board of seven top coaches. It's the first book to cover strategy extensively, a real lack in many books. Finally, each step of the way you will be learning the many drills you should do to become a top player. More than 120 drills are taught in this book.

A revolutionary approach to footwork is taken in this book. In most books on table tennis, footwork is taught at the very end, almost as an afterthought. Here, footwork is taught as it should be, as close to the beginning as possible. How can you hit a shot properly until you've learned to move into position?

Many have commented favorably on the strategy chapters taught here. There have been other books on table tennis, but none have adequately covered this subject. I've never understood why this was so, since strategy is so much a part of the game—more so than in almost any other sport. The hard part was limiting myself to just two chapters, plus many tactical suggestions in other sections. Someday I hope to write an entire book on tactics. As it is, the strategy sections are longer than some entire books on table tennis!

The section on advanced serves is, as far as I know, the first real description of advanced serves in print. Return of serve is covered extensively, from beginning to more advanced shots like the flip and short push.

Throughout this book, techniques are taught for right-handers. If you're left-handed, merely reverse accordingly, and please accept my apologies for not addressing you directly.

I would like to thank Human Kinetics Publishers (especially Dr. Judy Patterson Wright, my developmental editor, and Brian Holding, who helped get the whole thing started) for the help and advice they gave me. Without their help this book would not exist. I would like to thank Perry Malouf, Elaine Hodges, Dr. Lin, and Donna Sakai for taking the photos that the drawings are based on, and Sean O'Neill, Laura Lin, and Jennifer Newell, who served as the models for many of the photos. I would also like to thank Sean for the extensive editing and critiquing he did in the book's early drafts. I would like to thank Butterfly Table Tennis for their support of this project. And I would like to thank the United States Table Tennis Association and President Dan Seemiller for all their help and support, and especially the USTTA editorial board, which reviewed and made recommendations for the book.

Larry Hodges

The Steps to Success Staircase

Get ready to climb a staircase—one that will lead you to be a great table tennis player. You can't leap to the top; you get there one step at a time.

Each of the 15 steps you'll take is an easy transition from the one before. The first few steps of the staircase provide a solid foundation of basic skills and concepts. As you progress further, you'll learn how to connect groups of those seemingly isolated skills. Practicing combinations of table tennis skills will give you the experience you need to make natural and accurate decisions at the table. You'll learn to choose the proper stroke to match your particular table tennis needs—whether for quickness, power, deception, or just fun. As you near the top of the staircase, the climb will ease, and you'll find that you have developed a sense of confidence in your table tennis abilities that makes further progress a real joy.

To prepare to become a good climber, familiarize yourself with this and the following sections: "Table Tennis Today," "Table Tennis Equipment," and "Warming Up for Success." They'll orient you and show you how to set up your practice sessions.

Follow the same sequence each step of the way:

1. Read the explanations of what is covered in the step, why the step is important, and how to execute or perform the step's focus, which may be a basic skill, concept, or tactic, or combination of the three.
2. Follow the numbered illustrations showing exactly how to position your body to execute each basic skill. There are three general parts to each skill: preparation (getting into a starting position), execution (performing the skill), and follow-through (recovering to starting position). These are your "Keys to Success."
3. Look over the descriptions of common errors that may occur and the recommendations for how to correct them.
4. Read the directions and the Success Goal for each drill. Practice accordingly, record your score, and compare your score with the Success Goal. You should meet the Success Goal of each drill before moving on to the next, because the drills progress from easy to difficult. This sequence is designed to help you improve your skills through repetition and purposeful practice.
5. As soon as you reach all the Success Goals for one step, you are ready for a qualified observer—such as your teacher, coach, or training partner—to evaluate your basic skill technique by comparing them to the Keys to Success for each technique. This is a qualitative, or subjective, evaluation of your basic technique or form. Remember, using correct form will enhance your performance.
6. Go through these procedures for each of the 15 Steps to Success. Then rate yourself according to the directions for "Rating Your Total Progress."

Good luck in your step-by-step journey. You'll develop your table tennis skills, build confidence, be successful, and have fun!

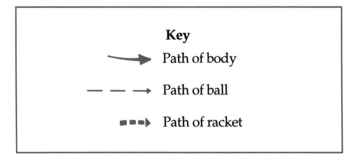

It's the most popular racket sport in the world and the second most popular participation sport. A sport with over 20 million active participants in the U.S. alone and, as of 1988, an Olympic sport. Ask most people to identify this sport and they'd immediately name that other well-known racket game. They'd be wrong.

You know what sport we are talking about or you wouldn't be looking at this book. Table tennis—never call it Ping-Pong except to other players!—has probably gotten the worst press of any comparable sport in the world. Many people think of it as, yes, Ping-Pong, a game where a small white ball is patted back and forth until someone misses. You and I know better. So do the many millions throughout the world who play the game competitively. Even in the U.S., more people play table tennis each year than soccer or baseball.

At the beginning level about all anybody does is just pat the ball back and forth. This is where its image as an easy sport probably came from, as it takes practice to learn to keep the ball going at a fast pace. But once learned it's a skill for life.

Table tennis is biggest in Asia and Europe. In the U.S. it is getting bigger very quickly. The United States Table Tennis Association (USTTA) has over 7,000 ranked tournament players and over 300 sanctioned clubs nationwide. Its Colorado Springs headquarters is staffed by eight full-time workers involved in everything from the running and sanctioning of tournaments and coaching camps to fund-raising and public relations. There are even two full-time coaches for the U.S. National and Olympic teams, as well as a number of other resident table tennis athletes.

Among other benefits, membership in the USTTA entitles you to play in any of the over 250 sanctioned tournaments in the U.S. each year. The largest and most prestigious is the U.S. Open held every June, with about 600 participants, including representatives from over 30 countries. There are also many other big tournaments, such as the U.S. Team Championships each November (with as many as 800 players) and the U.S. National Championships held each December. Membership also qualifies you to represent the U.S. in international play sponsored by the International Table Tennis Federation (ITTF), including the U.S. Open—if you're good enough. If you're not—well, that's why I wrote this book!

You'll also get the USTTA's magazine, *Table Tennis Today*. In it you'll find articles on everything from coaching to profiles, tournament writeups, results, and schedules. You'll also find the USTTA's rating list, a computerized ranking of all active tournament players. After you have played in a tournament, you too will be listed.

How do you join the USTTA? Contact the USTTA office for a general information packet and membership information. It will include full information on clubs, tournaments, and how to get involved in the fastest growing and most played racket sport (more so than tennis) in America! Here's the address:

USTTA
One Olympic Plaza
Colorado Springs, CO 80909
(719) 578-4583, (800) 326-USTT

Before you leap into the world of table tennis, you should know a few things about practicing. Although there are drills at the end of each section, they are directed toward beginning and intermediate players. You might find yourself practicing in a different environment.

METHODS OF PRACTICE

There are five methods of practicing table tennis, all of which have their advantages and disadvantages. You can choose the methods that best suit you.

- **Practicing with another player.** This will probably be your most common practice method, and it is usually the simplest. You and your partner can take turns choosing drills. It is assumed throughout this book that you have a practice partner.
- **Practicing with a coach.** This is probably the best way to practice, as you'll be able to concentrate on your weak points instead of taking turns with an opponent, and because you'll be getting coached at the same time. The disadvantage is that you have to find and possibly pay for a coach.
- **Practicing alone.** You can shadow-stroke the various shots and techniques without a ball. You can also get a bucket of balls and practice serves.
- **Multiball.** This is a method of practice for two players where one player practices while the other feeds. You'll need a bucket of balls. The feeder stands to the side of the table and picks up and hits the balls to you one at a time

in whatever speed, spin, and direction needed for you. This is an excellent way to learn shots, but it has the disadvantage that only one player can practice at a time. This method is often used by coaches, who do the feeding.

- **Robots.**   Owning a table robot is almost as good as having a person feed you multiball full time. Robots can be set for any speed, spin, or direction that you may wish. They can be expensive, but owning one gives you a tireless practice partner who never misses. Contact the USTTA for information on getting one.

To fully enjoy the sport of table tennis, you should know something about the sport itself, its history and rules.

A SHORT HISTORY OF TABLE TENNIS

The exact origin of table tennis is unknown. It began sometime in the 1890s as a parlor game and swept the country in a craze that soon died down.

It became popular again in the 1920s, and clubs were formed all over the world. The original name, Ping-Pong, was a copyrighted trademark of Parker Brothers, so the name was changed to table tennis. The International Table Tennis Federation (ITTF) was formed in 1926. The United States Table Tennis Association was formed in 1933.

As a parlor game the sport was often played with cork balls and vellum rackets. (A vellum racket had a type of rubber stretched on a twisted stick.) In the 1920s, wooden rackets covered with rubber "pips" were first used. These were the first hard rubber rackets, and they were the most popular type used until the 1950s.

During that time two playing styles dominated: hitters and choppers. Hitters basically hit everything while choppers would back up 10 or even 20 feet, returning everything with backspin. A player's attack with hard rubber was severely limited and so, more and more, choppers dominated. This became a problem whenever two choppers played each other: Both would often just push the ball back and forth for hours, waiting for the other to attack and make an error. This was stopped by the advent of the expedite rule. The rule helps players finish a game lasting longer than 15 minutes. From the time expedite is called, players alternate serves, and whoever serves must win the point within 13 shots, including the serve. Under expedite, an umpire counts the shots aloud and awards the point to the receiver if he or she returns 13 consecutive shots. This forces the server to play aggressively, while also ending long, boring rallies.

In 1952 a relatively unknown Japanese player named Hiroje Satoh showed up at the World Championships with a strange new type of racket. It was a wooden blade covered by a thick sheet of sponge. He easily won the tournament, and table tennis hasn't been the same since.

Over the next 10 years nearly all the top players switched to sponge coverings. Two types were developed: inverted and pips-out. The inverted type enabled players to put far more spin than was possible before, and both types made attacking and counterattacking far easier. The U.S., which was a table tennis power up until this time (the top seed at the 1952 World Championships was Marty Reisman of the U.S.) was slow to make the change, and by the 1960s was near the bottom of the world rankings.

In the early 1960s, players began to perfect sponge play. First they developed the loop shot (a heavy topspin shot), and soon looping became the most popular style. Spin serves were developed, as was the lob (a high, defensive return of a smash), the main weapon of 1967 World Champion Nobuhiko Hasegawa of Japan.

Japan dominated the game during the 1950s, mostly because its players were all using sponge. They also introduced the penhold grip, which gave them dominating forehands. China, at first using only the penhold grip but later the shakehands grip as well, began to dominate at the start of the 1960s. They dominated the game almost continuously until the 1989 World Championships where Sweden pulled off the upset of the decade, beating China 5-0 for the team championship. Both Men's Singles Finalists were Swedish, with Jan-Ove Waldner defeating Jorgen Persson three games to two. Sweden repeated at the next World Championships in 1991, this time beating Yugoslavia in the final. Waldner and Persson repeated as finalists, but this time Persson won, three games to zero. China dropped to seventh, but most tournament results show that they are back to being at least the second best in the world.

THE RULES

There are a number of misunderstandings and misconceptions about the rules of table tennis. The following are important points that should be noted. You might even want to make a copy of these rules and post them on the wall!

Scoring

- A player scores a point when an opponent fails to make a legal return. This includes hitting the ball off the end or side of the table, hitting into the net, or failing to make a good serve.

- A game is to 21 points. (Players often play practice games to 11.)
- A game must be won by 2 points.
- A match is best two out of three games, or best three out of five games.
- Serves are alternated every 5 points, except at deuce (20-20) when they are alternated every point.
- The game does not end at 7-0 or at any other score except 21 or deuce.

Serving

- The ball must be held in an uncupped hand, with the thumb free, fingers together.
- The ball must be tossed up at least 6 inches. The net is 6 inches high and can be used for comparison.
- The ball must be struck while it is dropping.
- Contact must be above the table level and behind the endline or its imaginary extension.

- Let serves (serves that nick the net but hit the other side of the table) are done over. You serve any number of let serves without losing a point.
- The ball must hit both sides of the table on a serve.

Rallying

- If you volley the ball (hit it before it bounces on your side of the table) you lose the point.
- The rally continues until someone fails to return the ball.
- If you move the table or touch it with your nonplaying hand, you lose the point.
- To start a game, one player hides the ball in one hand under the table and the other tries to guess what hand it is in. Winner gets the choice of serving or receiving first, or of which side to start on. You can also flip a coin.

Table Tennis Equipment

Four pieces of equipment are needed to play table tennis: the table, the net, the ball, and the racket. The racket is really two pieces of equipment—the racket itself and its covering. In addition, players must choose proper playing attire plus any of the many table tennis accessories available—table tennis glue, head and wrist bands, net measurer, racket holder and playing bag, and weighted rackets.

THE TABLE

The table is 9 feet by 5 feet, with the surface 30 inches from the floor. It is usually a dark, nonreflecting green, with a 3/4-inch white line running along the edge. There is also a 1/4-inch line running down the middle that is only used in doubles. (It doesn't invalidate the table for singles play.)

The way the ball bounces when it hits the table must meet certain standards. It should have a uniform bounce whether the ball is hitting near the edge or in the middle. It should bounce roughly the same on all legal tables. (When dropped from a height of 12 inches, the ball should bounce between 8-3/4 and 9-3/4 inches.) You won't be able to develop proper timing on a table that gives variable bounces. If at all possible, use tables that are either USTTA or ITTF approved.

Tables range from beat-up ones with gaping holes in the middle and bounces that defy gravity to thousand dollar ones that are scientifically designed. Try to use ones that are somewhere in between.

You'll need room to play. A legal playing court is at least 20 by 40 feet, but you may have to compromise on this depending on the size of your facility. Beginners don't need nearly as much room as more advanced players. If at all possible, the ceiling should be at least 12 feet or higher, but this isn't necessary for beginners. (You can't lob with a low ceiling, but lobbing is a rather advanced shot.)

The background should be dark enough so that the ball (usually white) can be seen clearly. Make sure there are no glares. Table tennis is a vision-oriented sport, and a white background or a glare from a window can ruin the game.

The floor should not be slippery, for obvious reasons. Most top players consider a wood floor (or something similar) best, because extensive play on a hard surface can hurt your feet and legs.

THE NET

The net is 6 inches high and stretches across the middle of the table. It should extend 6 inches on each side of the table—this is to keep players from hitting the ball around the net, something some top players can do.

If the net isn't the correct height you won't get a feel for proper ball trajectory. If you play with a net that is too low, you'll get in the habit of hitting the ball too low, and when you go to a regulation net, you'll hit into the net. If you play on a net that is too high, you'll hit the ball too high when you go to a regulation net.

Nothing is more irritating than a net that keeps falling over or that sags in the middle. Make sure the net being used is securely fastened and relatively taut.

THE BALL

Balls are usually white, but some are orange. They vary in price from cheap 10-cent balls that break on contact with a racket to three-star quality balls that cost nearly a dollar each. A poorly made ball tends to be lopsided, with soft spots, so that it not only breaks easily, it doesn't bounce the same way each time. You should probably go for the expensive three-stars. They bounce better, and in the long run they're cheaper because they last much longer. Balls are usually marked either one, two, or three-star. Get the three-stars. If there are no stars, avoid them.

THE RACKET

Choosing a racket consists of two parts. First you must choose the blade itself (a racket without the covering). Then you must choose the covering for the hitting surface. You'll want to pick the correct racket and covering for your particular style of play.

A blade is made of wood, although a small amount of carbon fiber or similar fibrous material is permitted. Most tournament players use plain wood but some use expensive (over $100) carbon fiber blades that give a more even bounce on different parts of the racket—a larger "sweet spot." Many players complain that carbon rackets have less "touch," which is why they are still less popular than plain wood.

When selecting a racket, you must consider your grip, playing style, price, and what feels comfortable. If you use the penhold grip (see Step 1, "Grip and Racket Control") then make sure to get a penhold racket.

Some beginners think it's "macho" or cool to use a fast blade. This is a mistake. A medium-speed blade will enable you to control the ball and develop your shots far more effectively. As you advance, you may want a faster blade if you develop an attacking style. If you develop a more defensive style, you may want a slower blade. The speed of most table tennis blades is usually marked on the package, ranging from "slow" to "very fast."

Ultimately, the deciding factor when selecting a blade (other than price) is the "feel." If it feels right, it's probably the best blade for you.

THE RACKET COVERING

The racket covering is even more important than the racket itself. There are five basic types: inverted, pips-out, hard rubber, long pips, and antispin. (Sandpaper and plain wood are also sometimes used, but they are illegal surfaces and should not be used. They were made illegal because they damage the ball.)

All racket coverings include a sheet of "pimpled" rubber, a sheet of rubber covered with conical "pips." These pips help grab the ball and put more spin on it.

Make sure to use some sort of sponge rubber covering (see Figure 1, a-c). A sponge racket is covered with a thin layer of sponge, with a pimpled rubber surface. There are basically three types of surfaces, two of which have sponge.

- Inverted sponge: The sheet of pimpled rubber is inverted. The pips face inward, toward the racket. This leaves a smooth surface. On some types of inverted sponge, the surface is sticky, which helps when spinning the ball but causes a loss of control. Sticky inverted is the best surface for putting spin on the ball, while less sticky inverted is best for all-around play. I recommend that beginners get a less sticky inverted surface.

- Pips-out sponge: Here the pips point outward. This type of surface is ideal for smashing but is not as good for spinning or all-around play. You can't spin the ball as well with this surface, but you have more control against spin.

- Hard rubber: Hard rubber is a sheet of pimpled rubber, pips outward, without any sponge under it. Before sponge rackets were invented in the 1950s, this was the most popular surface. A player with a sponge racket can keep the ball in play at a faster pace than with a hard rubber racket and can attack far more effectively. A player using hard rubber is at a severe disadvantage against an opponent with sponge, so I strongly recommend that you use a sponge of some sort.

Two other types of racket surfaces are occasionally used: "antispin rubber" and "long pips." These surfaces are different in their playing characteristics than other surfaces and are for special styles of play, mostly defensive. They will be covered in detail in Step 13, "Playing Styles and Rallying Tactics." I don't recommend these surfaces for beginners. As you learn more about the game, you may wish to try them out.

SPEED GLUES

Many top players now use some sort of speed glue, which makes the racket surface faster and "spinnier." The glue must be put on before each playing session because the effect wears off after a few hours. The glue adds a slingshot effect when hitting the ball, shooting the ball out. The effect only lasts until the glue hardens, which takes from 3 to 10 hours, depending on the type and the amount used.

Speed glue is especially useful for players who attack with topspin. The speed glue could more correctly be called "spin glue" because it really adds more spin than speed. Players who try speed glue usually have trouble controlling it at first, but they quickly adjust. Although speed glue does add more power to your game, it reduces your control.

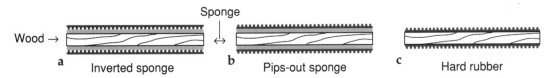

Figure 1 (a) Inverted sponge: a sheet of pimpled rubber is inverted. The pips face downward, toward the racket. (b) Pips-out sponge: the pips point outward. (c) Hard rubber: a sheet of pimpled rubber, pips outward, without any sponge underneath the rubber.

It is not recommended until players reach at least an intermediate level.

CARE OF YOUR EQUIPMENT

Table tennis equipment needs very little maintenance. However, if you use inverted sponge, you'll need to clean the racket surface. There are special rubber cleaners on the market that clean extremely well, but constant use of them will wear down the rubber. It's better to wash an inverted sponge with plain water and a towel. Use rubber cleaner mostly in tournaments.

All table tennis sponge wears out. The tiny bubbles in the sponge pop and eventually the sponge goes dead and should be replaced. The higher the level of play, the more often the sponge should be changed.

Inverted sponge surfaces also wear out, usually before the sponge does. If you like to spin the ball, you shouldn't use an old surface that is no longer grippy.

Sponge surfaces come in squares that have to be glued to the racket and cut. There are special table tennis glues for this, but you can also use rubber cement. The only disadvantage of rubber cement is that it is slightly thicker than table tennis glue and will create lumps under the surface if not put on properly.

You will need to know how to put on a fresh sheet of sponge. Here's how:

1. Apply a thin layer of glue to both the racket and sponge, and let it dry. (Bubbles may form under the sponge if you don't let it dry before continuing.)
2. Carefully put the sponge on the racket, starting at one end and rolling it over the surface.
3. Check the surface for bubbles. If there are any, squeeze them flat with either a roller of some sort or your fingers.
4. Put a piece of paper on the surface and then stack some books on top. Let it sit for 5 minutes or so.
5. Remove the books and cut away the excess sponge with scissors or razor blade.
6. Play!

SHOES AND CLOTHING

You should wear rubber-soled athletic shoes with athletic socks. Don't use running shoes; they're not designed for the sudden side to side movements needed in table tennis and can lead to sprained ankles. There are specially made table tennis shoes, but they aren't really necessary until you reach the higher levels. Volleyball shoes are ideal for table tennis.

Solid-colored, nonwhite shorts and shirts finish out your table tennis outfits, with warm-ups optional. (White outfits are illegal because an opponent can lose the ball against the white background. Likewise, orange clothing is illegal if an orange ball is used, in which case white clothes are legal.)

OTHER ACCESSORIES

There are a number of other items that you may choose to use. Here's a short list:

- Head and wrist bands
- Net measurer
- Racket holder
- Spare racket
- Playing bag
- Weighted racket, for shadow practice (or simply leave the cover on your regular racket)

Warming Up for Success

Many table tennis players go straight to the table when they want to play. Their muscles are cold and tight, and they not only can't play their best but can be injured before their muscles warm up. Before playing, you should warm up your muscles, stretch them, and go through some sort of table warm-up.

WHY IS WARMING UP IMPORTANT?

Warming up before play is important so you can play your best, and so you won't be injured. You can't possibly play as well with cold, tight muscles as with warm, loose ones. Any sudden unexpected move (a lunge for an edge ball, a sudden stretch to reach that ball to the wide forehand) can lead to injury. There are few things more frustrating than to sit on the sidelines with an injury.

Many players warm up at the table. This is better than nothing, but only a few specific muscles get warmed up that way. It just isn't enough. There should be four parts to your table tennis warm-up, as follows:

1. *Warming the muscles.* Start any playing session by some easy jogging or brisk walking to get the blood flowing into the muscles. This prepares your muscles for activity and warms them up so they are ready to be stretched.
2. *Stretching.* Now that your muscles are relatively warm, stretch the ones you will use the most (see next section). Use slow, easy stretches. Hold all stretches 6 to 8 seconds. To avoid injuries, never bounce when you stretch, and never stretch a cold muscle.
3. *Table warm-up.* Go through a routine that covers each shot that you may use. Now you're ready to play!
4. *Cool-down.* After you finish playing, your muscles are warm and flexible. This is the best time to stretch and to improve general flexibility.

WARMING THE MUSCLES

Jog around the playing area a few times. Don't go too fast—you don't want to injure yourself! All you want to do is get the blood flowing a little faster than normal and warm up the muscles. Later, when you've learned two-step footwork (Step 5), you can practice that slowly as a warm-up.

STRETCHING

Here is a modified version of the stretching routine used by the resident table tennis athletes at the Olympic Training Center at Colorado Springs. Feel free to vary it. On all stretches, move slowly through full range of motion.

Neck

Five-part Stretch: Stand tall with your back erect. Slowly drop your chin toward your chest. Hold for 1 second then bring your head back to its original position. Now let your head tilt to the right side. Hold for 6 to 8 seconds then bring your head erect again. Repeat on the left side. Finally, rotate your head to the right as if you are looking behind you. Hold for 6 to 8 seconds then bring your head erect again. Repeat on the left side.

Inhale as you bring your head back to the original position. Remember to only move your head, not your spine. Do each of these stretches 10 times.

Shoulders

Arm Circles: From a standing position, rotate both arms slowly forward in a circle. After circling forward for 10 rotations, change direction and circle both arms slowly backward 10 times. Inhale when you raise your arms and exhale when you lower them.

Wrist

Press and Extend: Slowly squeeze a rubber or tennis ball in your palm, then extend your fingers, 10 to 20 times. This helps to strengthen your wrist and forearm while also warming up your wrist for range-of-motion exercises.

Trunk/Back/Hips

Side Reach: Stand with your legs about shoulder-width apart while keeping your back straight. Reach high above your head with one arm while leaving the other dangling at your side. Feel the stretch in your side. Alternate on each side 10 times.

Trunk Twist: Sit with your back erect and your right leg straight in front of you. Bend your left leg, crossing it over your right leg. Rest your left foot flat on the floor outside of your right knee. Now slowly rotate your trunk, placing your right elbow outside of your left thigh. Place your left hand on the floor directly behind your buttocks. Push against your thigh with your right elbow and feel the stretch in your hips and your lower back. Perform the stretch on each side three times. Hold the position each time for 6 to 8 seconds.

Hamstrings

Sit and Reach: Sit on the floor with your right leg straight and the sole of your left foot touching the inside of your right thigh. Slowly bend forward from the hips and try to grasp your right foot with both hands. Stretch your arms as far as you can comfortably. You will feel tension in the back of your right thigh. Hold for 6 to 8 seconds, then release. Repeat the same exercise with the left leg extended. Perform the stretch three times on each leg.

Quadriceps

Stork Stand: Stand facing a wall. Extend your right arm and place it on the wall for balance. Bend your right leg and lift the foot toward your buttocks. Grab the foot with your left hand and gently pull the foot up and closer to your buttocks. You can feel the stretch in the front of your leg increase as you pull harder. Hold the stretch for 6 to 8 seconds then repeat the stretch with the left leg. You can further the stretch by bending forward at the waist.

Calves

Wall Lean: Stand facing a wall with your arms extended. Keeping your feet together and your knees straight, lean forward and feel the stretch in your calves. Hold for 6 to 8 seconds. Bend your knees, slightly round your back, and hold for 6 to 8 seconds. Remember to keep your heels on the floor and your feet parallel. Resume your stretch by lengthening your back and straightening your knees. Alternately repeat the stretches 10 times.

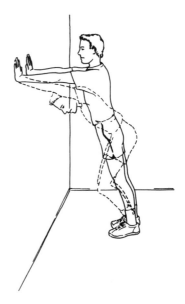

TABLE WARM-UP

If you don't recognize the drills mentioned, you will later as you go through this book. Depending on your playing style, you should vary this table warm-up—for example, a chopper would want to warm up using a chopping stroke. The following is a basic table warm-up sequence.

1. Hit forehand to forehand, crosscourt, 2 to 5 minutes.
2. Hit backhand to backhand, crosscourt, 2 to 5 minutes.
3. Hit forehand to backhand, down the line, 1 to 2 minutes on each line.
4. Do a side-to-side footwork drill, 2 to 5 minutes each.
5. Practice pushing all over, 2 to 5 minutes. Beginners should do backhand to backhand and forehand to forehand.
6. Loop forehands against block, 2 to 5 minutes each. Have your partner move you around a little bit. Then do the same with your backhand loop, if you have one.
7. Serve backspin, have partner push, and you attack. Play out the point, 2 to 5 minutes each.

After a table warm-up, you can either continue with a practice session or play matches.

COOL-DOWN

At the end of your practice or play, perform the same stretches you did before your table warm-up sequence. Now that your body is warmed up, you can easily improve your flexibility. You will find that your muscles may stretch more than they did before you started playing. Stretching them now will leave you even more flexible for your next game.

Step 1   Grip and Racket Control

How you play is determined in part by how you hold the racket. There are a limited number of standard grips, with an infinite number of variations. Once you've settled on which grip to use, you should use that grip for all shots.

These are the three basic grips:

- *Shakehands grip.* This grip is the most popular worldwide. It gives you the best all-around game as well as the best backhand. Currently among the best players, 9 of the top 10 (and 16 of the top 20) use the shakehands grip.
- *Penhold grip.* This is the second most popular grip. It gives you the best possible forehand but makes the backhand more difficult. A player using this grip should have very quick feet that enable her or him to play mostly forehand shots.
- *Seemiller grip.* This is a variation of the shakehands grip. With it you hit all shots with one side of the blade, leaving one side free as an alternate surface that can be used for surprise. This grip gives the best blocking game but has various technical weaknesses in both the forehand and backhand drives. These weaknesses show up mostly at the advanced level. This grip is for a player who has very quick hands and who likes to use deception (with the alternate surface).

Unless you already use or have a strong preference for a different grip, I recommend that you use the shakehands grip.

Throughout this book, I'll introduce all strokes initially for the shakehands grip. Most strokes are executed the same for the three grips, but wherever there is a difference, I'll have a separate section describing it.

WHY ARE PROPER GRIP AND RACKET CONTROL IMPORTANT?

As you progress in table tennis, you will see many variations in grips. But you'll find that the best players use only a few variations.

Most improper grips will not allow you to properly execute all the shots. For example, you may be able to hit a proper forehand with one improper grip but be unable, because of the body's mechanics, to hit a backhand properly. A poor grip will limit your game and your development.

After proper grip you need racket control. You have to be comfortable aiming the racket in different directions for different shots, adjusting racket angles to account for the incoming ball's speed, spin, and direction of flight. These little adjustments in racket control are the difference between keeping the ball in play and missing it.

SHAKEHANDS GRIP

The shakehands grip is the most versatile, the most popular, and the most recommended. Here is how to grip the racket, shakehands style:

1. With the blade perpendicular to the floor, grasp the racket as if you were shaking hands.
2. Extend your index finger along the bottom of the blade surface, with the thumb on the surface on the other side.

The thumb should be slightly bent and should rest so that the thumbnail is perpendicular to the hitting surface (the fleshy pad of the thumb is not touching the racket). The blade should rest in the crook of the thumb and forefinger, about a quarter-inch to the index-finger side, although this can be varied. The index finger should be near the bottom of the racket and not sticking up toward the tip. The thumb should not stick up on the racket too much (although some players do so to hit a backhand, switching back for the forehand).

With this grip you now have two anchors—the thumb and index finger, and the last three fingers around the handle. Also, the blade should rest on the middle finger for further support. With these anchors in place, the blade is very stable.

Your thumb is resting on the *forehand side* of the racket (Figure 1.1a); your index finger is on the *backhand side* (Figure 1.1b).

When you're hitting a backhand, the thumb gives the racket a firm backing; for a forehand, the index finger does this. This, along with the two anchors, creates good racket control.

Most people find a compromise between the forehand and backhand grips by holding it somewhere in between, which is called a neutral grip (Figure 1.1c). But it is important to distinguish between both types of rotation. If, while holding the racket in front of you (in a shakehands grip), you rotate the top of the blade toward you, then you'll have more power and control on the forehand side (Figure 1.1d), and the reverse for the backhand. If you rotate the top of the racket away from you, you'll have a backhand grip (Figure 1.1e). This will give you more power and control on the backhand side, but does the reverse for the forehand. Generally, I don't recommend changing grips in a rally, but some players do so.

Shakehands Grip

Strengths

- Most versatile grip

- Only grip that allows an effective backhand loop (see Step 8)
- Best grip for backhand
- Best grip for off-the-table play
- Best grip for defensive play
- Very strong on shots to the corners

Weaknesses

- Weak against shots to the middle
- Difficult to use wrist on some shots

Figure 1.1   *Keys to Success:*
Shakehands Grip

**Preparation
Phase**

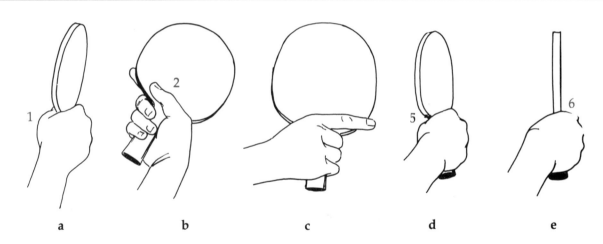

a   b   c   d   e

1. Blade rests in crook between thumb and forefinger ____
2. Thumbnail perpendicular to racket surface ____
3. Index finger near bottom of racket ____
4. Loose grip ____
5. To strengthen forehand, rotate top of racket toward you ____
6. To strengthen backhand, rotate top of racket away from you ____
7. For best balance of forehand and backhand, grip somewhere in between. You should be closer to Figure 1.1a. ____

Detecting Shakehands Grip Errors

Players can play reasonably well with an incorrect grip. However, many matches will then revolve around players' attempts to compensate for any weaknesses in their grip. If you start out with a correct grip you will have an advantage. So, make sure you aren't guilty of any of the following errors.

ERROR

CORRECTION

1. Either your forehand or backhand shots feel erratic or unstable.

1. Rotating the top of the racket forward (when holding the racket in front of the body with a shakehands grip) will make the backhand more stable but the forehand less stable; rotating it backward will do the reverse. Most players find a compromise between the two extremes.

2. The soft part of your thumb touches the racket.

2. This gives you an erratic forehand as well as less power on the backhand. Your thumbnail should be perpendicular to the racket. Review Figure 1.1.

3. Your index finger sticks out onto the surface on backhand side of the racket.

3. This gives a good forehand, but an unstable backhand. It also gives less hitting area for the backhand. Keep your index finger near the bottom of the blade.

4. Your grip is too tight.

4. Relax your grip. Holding the racket too tightly costs you both power and control. A good way to tell if you're holding the racket too tightly is to imagine someone sneaking up behind you as you play and grabbing your racket. If the person would have trouble pulling it from your grip, you are holding the racket too tightly.

PENHOLD GRIP

The penhold grip gives the best possible forehand but the weakest backhand. You should only use it if you're very quick on your feet, because players with this grip are often forced to use the forehand from the backhand side to compensate for the weaker backhand. There are, of course, exceptions to this, but a penholder who is slow on his or her feet usually will not be able to do more than keep the ball in play with his or her backhand.

With the penhold grip, one side of the racket is used for all shots. The other side may have an alternate hitting surface but the nature of the grip makes it hard to switch in the middle of a rally. Here is how to hold the racket, penhold style:

1. Hold the racket upside down, handle up (Figure 1.2a). Grasp the racket where the handle meets the blade with your thumb and forefinger. This is similar to holding a pen (hence the name).
2. Either curl the other three fingers on the other side of the blade (Chinese penhold grip, see Figure 1.2b) or extend them straight down the back of the racket, fingers together (Korean penhold grip, see Figure 1.2c).

With both versions of this grip, the racket is held between the three fingers on the back and the thumb and index finger on the front. The three fingers on the back give the racket a firm backing on all shots.

Note that with this grip, the forehand and the backhand side of the racket are the same because only one side of the racket is used to hit the ball.

Penhold Grip

Strengths

- Best possible forehand
- Quick backhand
- Easy to use wrist on most shots, especially serves
- No center weakness

Weaknesses

- Backhand somewhat cramped, more limited
- Not as good for defensive shots except blocking
- Backhand weak away from table

Figure 1.2   Keys to Success: *Penhold Grip*

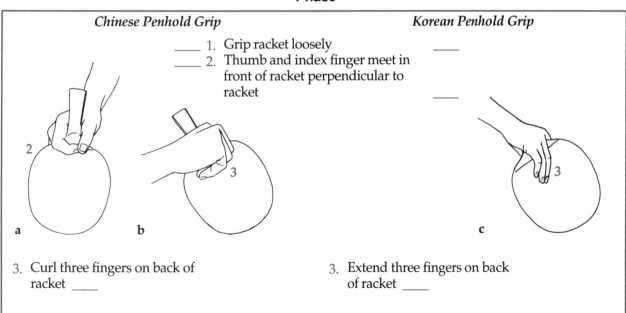

Preparation Phase

Chinese Penhold Grip   *Korean Penhold Grip*

_____ 1. Grip racket loosely   _____
_____ 2. Thumb and index finger meet in front of racket perpendicular to racket

a   b   c

3. Curl three fingers on back of racket _____

3. Extend three fingers on back of racket _____

Detecting Penhold Grip Errors

If you choose to use the penhold grip it is important you master it. Otherwise you may be at a disadvantage. Try to avoid the following errors.

ERROR

CORRECTION

1. Either your forehand or your backhand grip feels weak or erratic.

1. Rotate the right side of the racket forward to make your forehand stronger (see Figure a); rotate the right side of the racket backward to make your backhand stronger (see Figure b). It's usually best to compromise between the two with a neutral grip (see Figure c).

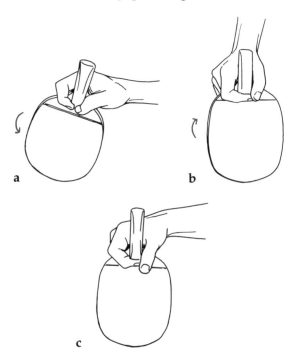

2. Your grip is too tight.

2. See number 4 under "Detecting Shakehands Grip Errors."

SEEMILLER GRIP

The Seemiller grip, also known as the American grip, is a version of the shakehands grip. It has been used for many years, but it was first used successfully in the 1970s and 1980s by five-time U.S. National Champion Dan Seemiller. Some coaches consider it an inferior grip because they believe that you cannot have both a good forehand and a good backhand with it, but many disagree. If you already use the grip, you don't need to switch. Just make sure to do it correctly.

As with the penhold grip, only one side of the racket is used for striking the ball. This gives an alternate hitting surface that you can use in the middle of a rally by flipping the racket. Most players using the Seemiller grip use inverted sponge on one side and antispin sponge on the other.

Here's how to hold the racket, Seemiller style:

1. Grip the racket with a shakehands grip.
2. Rotate the top of the racket from 20 to 90 degrees toward you, see Figure 1.3a. (The more you rotate, the stronger your backhand shots will be and the weaker the forehand, and vice versa.)
3. Curl the index finger around the edge of the racket, see Figure 1.3b.

With this grip, the racket is held by two anchors: The index finger and thumb hold the racket face itself between them, and the racket handle is held by the last three fingers.

Because you're using only one hitting surface (except when you flip the racket), the hitting surface usually will face your opponent. So, your thumb will be facing your opponent. This gives the effect of a windshield-wiper motion when going from the backhand to the forehand shot, and vice versa. Try it and you'll see. (With this grip, like the penhold grip, the forehand and backhand side of the racket are the same.)

Seemiller Grip

Strengths

- Gives a player an excellent blocking game
- Allows player an alternate surface to use as a variation
- No center weakness
- Allows a lot of wrist motion on many shots, especially the forehand loop

Weaknesses

- Weak against well-angled shots
- Depending on how racket is rotated either forehand or backhand can feel awkward, especially on shots to the wide corners
- Generally not as good for defensive shots, except blocking
- Backhand weak away from table

Figure 1.3   *Keys to Success: Seemiller Grip*

Preparation Phase

1. Point thumb in same direction as hitting surface ____
2. Index finger touches racket only on the edge ____
3. Loose grip ____

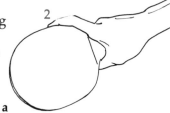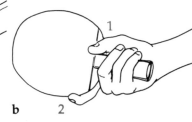

a   b

Detecting Seemiller Grip Errors

If you choose the Seemiller grip, it will be to your advantage to do it correctly and with strength. Avoid the following errors by following the correction illustrations.

ERROR   **CORRECTION**

1. Either your forehand or your backhand grip feels weak or erratic.

1. Rotate the top of the racket forward to make your forehand stronger (see Figure a); rotate the top of the racket backward to make your backhand stronger (see Figure b). It's usually best to compromise between the two with a neutral grip.

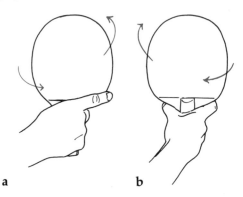

a   b

2. Your grip is too tight.

2. See number 4 under "Detecting Shakehands Grip Errors."

RACKET CONTROL

You could start practicing ball control right away at the table with an opponent, but at the start you want a slightly more predictable environment. A good way to develop faster is with ball bouncing (see Figure 1.4).

Figure 1.4   Practice bouncing a ball up and down on your racket.

Ball bouncing allows you to hit a ball that is moving more predictably than it would in a normal rally. It enables you to learn to hit the ball with the center of the racket consistently (the "sweet spot"). Just bounce a ball up and down on your racket, learning to hit the sweet spot every time. This will help you later when you start practicing at the table. There will be several drills involving ball bouncing in the drills section.

Much of your racket control is done by the wrist. Many players hold their rackets too firmly in their hands. This takes away wrist snap (and therefore power) and reduces your ability to easily change racket angles. It is important to always hold the racket rather loosely and relaxed.

A general rule about using the wrist in table tennis shots is this: If the incoming ball is traveling slowly, use more wrist. If it's traveling fast, use less or none. Some players use wrist in nearly all their shots, but that can be difficult to control.

Grip and Racket Control Drills

Note: For all drills, you should use the grip you have chosen. You may, however, use the drills to help decide which grip is most comfortable for you. You don't need a table to practice the following drills.

1. Up-and-Down Bouncing

The purpose of this drill is to learn to hit the ball in the center of the racket consistently. This will develop your awareness of the sweet spot that you will later use to your advantage in an actual rally. Using your normal grip, bounce the ball on the forehand side of the racket as many times in a row as you can, about a foot high each time. Try to make the ball hit the sweet spot every time. Then try to do the same thing with the backhand side of the racket.

Success Goal = 30 consecutive bounces on each side of the racket

Your Score =

(#) _____ consecutive forehand bounces

(#) _____ consecutive backhand bounces

2. Up-and-Down Wrist Bouncing

The purpose of this drill is to learn to control the racket with the wrist, again to enhance your ability to do so in an actual rally. Hold your racket hand just above the wrist with your free hand, so that you can only move the racket with your wrist. Don't move your arm during this drill! Using only the wrist, redo the previous drill.

Success Goal = 8 consecutive bounces on each side of the racket, using only wrist

Your Score =

(#) _____ consecutive forehand bounces

(#) _____ consecutive backhand bounces

3. Alternate Bouncing

Bounce the ball on the racket, this time alternating between hitting with the forehand and the backhand side. This will help you learn to hit the ball in the center of the racket while moving the paddle about, as you will have to do in a rally.

Success Goal = 30 consecutive alternating bounces

Your Score = (#) _____ consecutive alternating bounces

4. Wall Bouncing

Using the backhand side of your racket, bounce a ball against a wall as many times in a row as you can. Stand about 2 to 5 feet away from the wall and do not let the ball hit the floor. Hit the ball with a backhand stroke, facing the wall; hit the ball directly in front of your body. Try to make the ball hit the same spot on the wall each time, about shoulder height. (You might want to draw a chalk line to give yourself a target.) Consistency is especially important here—don't hit one shot shoulder-high, and the next way above your head. You're learning to do a repeating shot—the same stroke over and over. If you mis-hit a shot in this drill, the return from the wall will be off and you'll have trouble keeping the "rally" going. Try to develop a rhythm, hitting your shots the same way, over and over, always in the center of the racket. Next, try to do this with the forehand side of the racket, hitting the ball with a forehand stroke. Contact should be to the right of the body (for right-handers).

Success Goal = 15 consecutive wall bounces on each side of the racket, hitting the same spot

Your Score =
   (#) _____ consecutive backhand wall bounces
   (#) _____ consecutive forehand wall bounces

5. *Pepper*

This drill is named after a similar baseball drill. One player tosses a ball at a partner randomly, side to side. The other player has to hit each ball back at the tosser, who catches the ball and immediately tosses it again. The tosser shouldn't throw the ball too hard or too far away—the ball should stay within reach of the hitter. The hitter hits the ball after it has bounced once on the ground, not on the fly. The hitter shouldn't hit the ball hard. The purpose is to develop ball control, so the goal is to hit the ball as accurately as possible to the tosser. In this drill you'll learn to adjust to a moving ball and hit it where you want to. Make sure you always hit the ball in the center of your racket.

Success Goal = 15 consecutive accurate returns by the hitter

Your Score = (#) _____ consecutive accurate returns

Grip and Racket Control
Keys to Success Checklists

Developing racket control now will make it far easier for you later on when you are trying new techniques. In this section you have learned how to grip the racket and control it. A good grip will save you from endless headaches later on, while racket control will help you learn each step more quickly.

Use the proper Keys to Success checklists (see Figures 1.1 through 1.3) to decide which grip you are going to use. Ask the observer to verify if you can consistently bounce the ball in the center of the racket. Have your coach, instructor, or practice partner use the checklists to critique your grip and racket control.

Step 2   Spin and Racket Angles: It's a Game of Spin

Table tennis is a game of spin. Nearly every stroke and serve imparts some type of spin to the ball, and to understand them you have to understand each type of spin.

WHY IS SPIN IMPORTANT?

All good players put spin on their shots. An attacker uses topspin to control her or his attack, a defender uses backspin to control his or her defense. Nearly all players use sidespin on their serves to keep their opponents from making a strong return. Without spin, the game would be very different and a lot less exciting.

Because your opponents will be using spin, you must also. The types of spins you use against various shots will depend on what type of style you develop. But it's a given that if you wish to develop your game fully, you must learn how to use spin and how to play against it. To do this, you must first understand the various types of spins.

There are three basic types of spin: topspin, backspin, and sidespin (see Figure 2.1). You can use combinations of them, or use no spin at all ("no-spin").

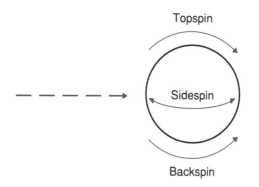

Figure 2.1   The three basic types of spin.

TOPSPIN

If you hit the ball so that the top half of it rotates away from you, you create topspin. This is done by hitting the back of the ball (usually toward the top) with an upward stroke.

Characteristics of topspin:

- The ball travels in a downward arc (see Figure 2.2). This means that a hard-hit ball that would normally go off the end of the table can still hit the table. This makes topspin ideal for attackers because you can control the attack by forcing the ball down.
- The ball jumps after it hits the table, throwing off an opponent's timing and making it difficult to return. This may cause the opponent to miss the return because the opponent cannot adjust.
- The ball will be returned high or off the end of the table if the spin is not taken into account.

Some players go for excessive spin, using topspin as a weapon by itself. This type of player is a *looper*. Others use just enough topspin to control their hard-hit drives. This type of player is a *hitter*. In general, the stronger a player is, the more he or she is physically suited to looping. The quicker a player is, the more he or she is suited to hitting. However, serious players need to do both.

BACKSPIN

If you hit the ball so that the bottom half of it rotates away from you, you create backspin (also known as underspin or chop). This is done by hitting the back of the ball (usually toward the bottom) with a downward stroke.

Characteristics of backspin:

- The ball travels in a line (see Figure 2.2). This keeps the ball at the same height for a longer period of time than other balls, which makes it easier to keep the ball low. This makes backspin ideal for defensive players. (Actually, backspin makes the ball curve upward—but this is balanced out by gravity pulling the ball down, so the ball tends to go in a line.)
- The ball will be returned into the net if the spin is not taken into account.
- The ball will slow down after it hits the table, throwing off an opponent's timing and making it difficult to return.

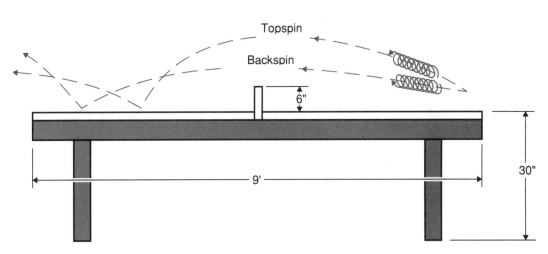

Figure 2.2   Differences between topspin and backspin ball arcs.

- A good backspin serve usually will keep an opponent from attacking the serve, often forcing a backspin return that can be attacked.

Backspin is used primarily as a defensive or passive shot. It's used to keep the ball low and difficult to attack. Some defensive players ("choppers") will back up 15 feet or more to return topspin drives with backspin. Backspin can lead to pushing, which is returning a ball that has backspin with your own backspin.

SIDESPIN

If you hit the ball so that the side of it moves away from you, you create sidespin. This is done by hitting the back of the ball (usually toward the side) with a sideways stroke. The ball spins like a record on a record player.

Characteristics of sidespin:

- The ball curves sideways. This can throw off an opponent's timing.
- The ball will bounce sideways when it hits the table, throwing off an opponent's timing and making it difficult to return.
- The ball will be returned off to the side if the spin is not taken into account.
- Sidespin is especially effective on serves. A good sidespin serve can force an opponent into an error.

NO-SPIN

A ball without spin is also a good variation, especially on the serve.

Characteristics of no-spin:

- Unless the ball is very low, it can be attacked easily if read properly.
- A short no-spin ball will often be mistaken for backspin, with the result that it is popped up; or it can be mistaken for topspin or sidespin and put in the net.
- Any spin shot can be done without spin as a variation.

RACKET ANGLES AGAINST SPIN: CLOSED AND OPEN

When your racket is pointing downward, so that the top of the racket is tilted away from you, the racket is closed. When your racket is pointing upward, so that the top of the racket is tilted toward you, it's open. Your racket angle will vary according to your position and shot and the incoming ball's spin and speed.

At first, you may have trouble returning spin. But you can quickly learn to adjust your racket angle to compensate. Here's how:

- To return a topspin, the racket must be closed (see Figure 2.3).
- To return a backspin, the racket must be open (see Figure 2.4).
- To return a sidespin, the racket must turn the opposite way that the ball is coming.

Generally, if you hit the ball off the end of the table, your racket is too open. If you hit the ball into the net, your racket is too closed.

Figure 2.3   Keep your racket closed to return a topspin ball.

Figure 2.4   Keep your racket open to return a backspin ball.

CREATING SPIN

Maximum spin is produced by just grazing the ball. The more the ball is grazed and the faster the racket is moving at contact, the more spin there will be. If you contact the ball toward the tip of the racket, you'll also get more spin, because the racket tip moves faster than the rest of the racket in nearly all shots. The tip is the part of the hitting surface farthest from the handle.

To achieve maximum spin, you should use a "grippy" inverted rubber. But beware that the grippier the surface is, the more a spinning ball will take on it, and the harder it will be to return a spinning ball. Beginners are urged to use only a moderately grippy surface.

The opposite of grazing the ball is hitting it "flat." If you hit the ball flat, that means the ball sinks straight into the sponge. The ball should hit the racket in a near perpendicular line and shoot out with only light spin, usually a light topspin. The basic forehand and backhand drives are both flat shots.

Detecting Errors Against Spin

One of the most common and basic errors in table tennis is misreading spin. For example, if your shot goes into the net, there probably was either more backspin or less topspin than you thought—so open your racket. A ball that doesn't go where you aim it is a symptom. Reading spin (and adjusting your racket angle) is the cure. You must watch how the racket contacts the ball and judge whether it hit it solidly or just grazed, how fast the grazing motion was, and in what direction. The faster the racket speed, and the more it grazes the ball, the more spin it will have. You will have to adjust to the spin accordingly. Practice and precision will help you improve as well as the following tips.

ERROR    **CORRECTION**

1. You return opponent's backspins into the net.	1. Open your racket more and aim higher. Read degree of spin—see 4 below.
2. You return opponent's topspins off the end.	2. Close your racket more and aim lower. Read degree of spin—see 4 below.
3. You return opponent's sidespins off to the side.	3. Make sure you're reading which type of sidespin your opponent is using, and aim in the opposite direction that the ball is coming. Read degree of spin—see 4 below.
4. You misread the amount of spin on the incoming ball.	4. Watch your opponent's racket just before and after contact. Try to judge racket speed at contact and speed of the incoming ball. Racket speed converts to speed and spin, so the slower the incoming ball is (relative to racket speed), the more spin it has. Also take into account your opponent's racket surface—grippy surfaces transmit spin more efficiently. Watch the ball carefully as its arc can also tell you how much spin it has—topspins drop quickly, backspins float.

Spin and Racket Angles Drills

1. Topspin Usage

Pretend you are playing a fast-paced game of table tennis. Your opponent gives you a backspin shot. You decide to return the ball using topspin. What are three possible outcomes of using topspin? (Refer to the characteristics of topspin discussed earlier in this step.)

Success Goal = Identify 3 outcomes of using topspin

a. _____

b. _____

c. _____

Your Score = (#) _____ outcomes of using topspin

2. *Backspin Usage*

Imagine you are playing a practice game. Your opponent serves backspin. You decide to return the ball using backspin. What are three possible outcomes of using backspin? (Refer to the characteristics of backspin discussed earlier in this step.)

Success Goal = Identify 3 outcomes of using backspin

    a. _____

    b. _____

    c. _____

Your Score = (#) _____ outcomes of using backspin

3. *Sidespin Usage*

Pretend you are still playing your practice game. You decide to serve sidespin. What are two possible outcomes of using sidespin? (Refer to the characteristics of sidespin discussed earlier in this step.)

Success Goal = Identify 2 outcomes of using sidespin

    a. _____

    b. _____

Your Score = (#) _____ outcomes of using sidespin

4. *No-Spin Serve*

Pretend you and your opponent are tied. You decide to fool your opponent by using a no-spin serve. What could be two possible outcomes? (Refer to the characteristics of no spin discussed earlier in this step.)

Success Goal = Identify 2 outcomes of serving with no spin

    a. _____

    b. _____

Your Score = (#) _____ outcomes of using no spin

5. Producing Topspin and Backspin

Away from the table, toss the ball up and hit it with the forehand motion. (If you do it against a wall, it'll bounce back to you so you can catch it and do it again.) Graze the ball at contact with an upward motion to produce topspin. Don't worry where the ball goes right now. Repeat, producing a backspin with a downward grazing motion. Next, use a backhand motion first with an upward grazing motion, then with a downward grazing motion.

Success Goal = Put topspin on the ball at least 10 times with both the forehand and backhand side of your racket; do the same with backspin

Your Score =

(#) _____ topspins with a forehand motion

(#) _____ backspins with a forehand motion

(#) _____ topspins with a backhand motion

(#) _____ backspins with a backhand motion

6. Racket Angles

Pretend you are playing a game, and you want to practice returning topspin, backspin, and sidespin. When preparing your returns you must think of how you will angle your racket. List the three different racket angles you would use for returning topspin, backspin, and sidespin.

Success Goal = Identify 1 angle for topspin, 1 angle for backspin, and 1 angle for sidespin

a. _____

b. _____

c. _____

Your Score = (#) _____ angles correctly identified to adjust to different spins

7. Producing Sidespin

Toss a ball up about a foot or two and hit it with either side of your racket with a sideways grazing motion to produce sidespin. The ball should bounce sideways when it hits the floor. Draw a target on the floor about 3 feet from a wall. Stand about 3 feet from the wall and hit the ball so that it travels parallel to the wall until the sidespin makes it curve around the target and hit the wall.

Success Goal = Curve the ball around a target at least 10 times

Your Score =

(#) _____ sidespins with forehand side of racket

(#) _____ sidespins with backhand side of racket

8. Backspin Return Drill

Away from the table, toss the ball up and stroke it with a grazing motion to produce backspin. (Make sure to contact the bottom of the ball with a very open racket.) The ball should hit the floor and, after a few bounces, either come to a stop or, if it has good backspin, bounce or roll back toward you. Draw a line on the ground with chalk (or use a line that's already on the floor) and try serving so the ball passes the line and comes back across it. (If you have trouble making the ball come back, try to make the ball at least come to a stop, and count that as your success goal.) If you have a partner, see who can make the ball come back the most.

Try another contest to see who can make the ball come back the most, with the ball having to bounce at least once past the line before coming back. Each player gets five tries, and the ball that comes back past the line the most wins.

Success Goal = Make the ball go past the line on the floor and come back at least 5 times

Your Score = (#) _____ times you make ball go past the line and then return

Spin and Racket Angles Summary

In this step you have learned how to produce topspin, backspin, sidespin, and no-spin. You have also learned how to angle your racket (closed, open, side) in order to return a topspin, a backspin, and a sidespin, respectively. By knowing how to create and read spin, you can adjust to your opponent's maneuvers and better control the game.

Answers to Step 2 Drills

Topspin Usage (#1)

  a. You can control your attack.

  b. You can force a miss because your opponent can't adjust to the ball's bounce in time.

  c. You can force your opponent to return the ball high or off the table.

Backspin Usage (#2)

  a. You can keep the ball low so it barely arcs over the net.

  b. You can force a miss because your opponent doesn't adjust to the ball's bounce in time.

  c. You can force your opponent to return the ball into the net.

Sidespin Usage (#3)

  a. You can force a miss because your opponent can't adjust to the ball's bounce in time.

  b. You can set up your next shot by forcing your opponent to return to one side or completely offside.

No-Spin Serves (#4)

  a. Your opponent could return the ball high if he or she thinks the ball has backspin.

  b. Your opponent could return the ball into the net if he or she thinks the ball has topspin.

Racket Angles (#6)

  a. Close your racket against topspin.

  b. Open your racket against backspin.

  c. Turn your racket to the opposite direction that the ball is coming for sidespin.

Step 3 Ready Stance and the Forehand and Backhand Drives

Before you can properly execute any table tennis shot, you need to learn a correct ready position. You'll learn that in this step. You'll also learn the forehand and backhand drives, the backbone of your game. The drive is an aggressive topspin shot.

The forehand drive is generally the strongest shot in the game, because, unlike the backhand, the body is not in the way during the shot. Also, the muscles used in the shot are generally better developed than those used in the backhand. The forehand smash, which is simply a forehand drive at full speed, will likely become your most powerful shot. It's done pretty much the same way with all three grips.

The backhand can be done against backspin, but it's usually better against topspin. It's usually not as powerful as the forehand (although it can be), and so consistency and quickness are generally more important. The backhand is done differently with all three grips. I'll also cover the smash, which is simply a very hard backhand or forehand.

WHY ARE THE DRIVES IMPORTANT?

The forehand drive (an aggressive topspin shot) is important for three reasons. First, you need it to attack shots to your forehand side. Second, it will probably be your primary attacking shot. Third, it's the shot you'll use most often to smash. Forehand shots are generally stronger than backhand shots, because the body is not in the way when you backswing and the muscles used are generally stronger.

The backhand complements your forehand in covering the table. It is needed to return drives to your backhand side and is used to force errors with quick returns. As your backhand gets better, you can use it more aggressively. Many players have weak backhands, so if you can learn to attack strongly with your backhand, you'll have a big advantage. Jan-Ove Waldner and Jorgen Persson of Sweden, the 1989 and 1991 World Men's Singles Champions, won on the strength of their attacks from both sides. Try to develop the backhand and forehand equally, or your opponent will always have a weak side to play to. Some players have had great success by making the backhand their main

power shot; they often win matches because their opponents simply aren't used to playing someone with a good backhand.

READY STANCE

Imagine a top tennis player standing flatfooted and slouching, but attempting to hit a strong forehand. She'd either hit a very weak shot or fall flat on her face!

The same goes for table tennis. You can't hit a strong shot unless you have a good stance. You have to be well balanced and coiled like a spring (see Figure 3.1).

Figure 3.1   Ready stance.

Most players automatically stand facing the endline (i.e., their feet point perpendicular to the line at the edge of the table that is called the endline). This is correct for players who favor their backhand, but most advanced players either favor the forehand or play both sides equally, and for them the proper stance is with the right foot slightly back, but the body still facing the table (or incoming ball). This puts you in a good position to hit either a backhand or a forehand. Your weight should be on the inside balls of the feet, evenly distributed. Try not to let your heels touch the ground. Your knees should be bent, with your body in a slight crouch. The taller you are, the more you need to bend your knees. This brings you down to the playing surface and enables you to spring in either direction very quickly.

Your racket should point at your opponent. This allows you to move it in both directions equally and quickly. Use your free hand as a counterbalance. It shouldn't just hang there! Keep your wrist above your elbow at all times.

Now relax. No hunched shoulders or clenched teeth or fists allowed! But don't relax *too* much; don't slouch. It's unnecessary tenseness that should be eliminated.

EXECUTING THE FOREHAND DRIVE

Start out facing the table, your right foot slightly back (see Figure 3.2a). Rotate your body to the right at the waist, with the hand swinging outward. Keep your elbow near your waist. Rotate your weight to your right foot. During the backswing, keep the racket perpendicular to the floor. The racket tip and arm should point slightly down, with your elbow at about 120 degrees (see Figure 3.2b).

Start the forward swing by rotating your weight forward onto your left foot. At the same time, rotate your waist and arm forward, keeping your elbow almost stationary. Elbow angle should decrease to about 90 degrees (see Figure 3.2c). Backswing and forward swing should be one continuous motion.

Make contact at about the top of the bounce, in front and slightly to the right of your body. The racket should rotate around the top and back of the ball, creating topspin. For a hard-hit forehand or against topspin, the racket should be closed and contact on the back of the ball toward the top. For a softer forehand, or against backspin, the racket should be open and contact more under the ball. Against backspin, stroke slightly up. Make sure to "stroke through" the ball—do not stop at contact;

use the upward and forward motion of the racket to sink the ball into the sponge.

Follow through with the racket going roughly to your forehead or a little to the left, similar to a salute. Taller players should follow through lower, shorter players a little higher. Your weight should be transferred to the left leg, with your shoulders and trunk rotated to the left (see Figure 3.2d). Return to the ready position.

EXECUTING THE BACKHAND DRIVE

Rotate your forearm toward your waist (see Figure 3.2, a and b). Racket and arm should point sideways, with your elbow at about 90 degrees. During the backswing, the racket should be perpendicular against topspin, slightly open against backspin. Keep your elbow stationary.

Start the forward swing by rotating your forearm forward. Move your elbow forward just enough to keep the racket going in a straight line (see Figure 3.2c).

At contact, snap your wrist forward and over the ball, closing the racket. The racket rotates around the ball, creating topspin (see Figure 3.2d). For extra power, stroke straight through the ball with less spin, sinking the ball straight into the sponge and wood. For a hard-hit backhand, or against topspin, the racket should be closed. For a softer backhand, or against backspin, the racket should be open. Against backspin, stroke slightly up.

Extend your arm forward and slightly up, with your elbow extending forward to keep the racket going in a straight line until the very end of the follow-through. At the end of the stroke, the racket should point a little to the right of the direction the ball was hit. Your arm should be almost fully extended.

Figure 3.2   *Keys to Success:*
Forehand and Backhand Drives

Preparation Phase

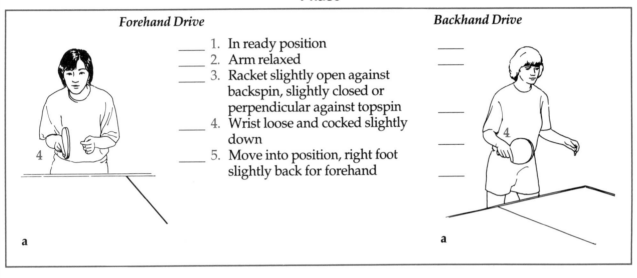

Forehand Drive   *Backhand Drive*

____ 1. In ready position
____ 2. Arm relaxed
____ 3. Racket slightly open against backspin, slightly closed or perpendicular against topspin
____ 4. Wrist loose and cocked slightly down
____ 5. Move into position, right foot slightly back for forehand

a   a

Execution Phase

Backswing

Forehand Drive   *Backhand Drive*

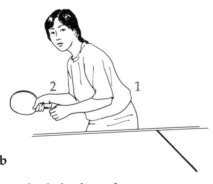

b   b

1. Rotate body backward at waist and hips ____
2. Rotate arm backward at elbow ____
3. Rotate weight to back foot ____
4. Against backspin, racket should start out slightly lower ____

1. Bring racket straight toward the waist ____
2. Against underspin, bring racket slightly down ____
3. Cock wrist backward ____
4. Racket perpendicular, or slightly closed, against topspin; slightly open against backspin ____

Forward Swing

Forehand Drive

c

1. Rotate weight to front foot ____
2. Rotate body forward on waist and hips ____
3. Rotate arm forward from the elbow ____
4. Contact made in front and to the right side of body ____

Backhand Drive

c

1. Racket moves straight forward ____
2. Elbow moves slightly forward ____
3. Contact made in front and slightly to left side ____
4. Turn top of wrist down at contact so it faces the table, closing the racket ____

Follow-Through Phase

Forehand Drive

d

1. Racket goes forward and slightly up naturally ____
2. Return to ready position ____

Backhand Drive

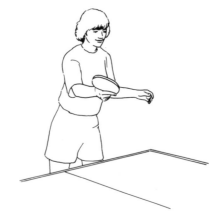

d

1. Racket goes in general direction ball is hit ____
2. Return to ready position ____

BACKHANDS WITH OTHER GRIPS

When doing a backhand with the Seemiller grip, remember that you use the same side of the racket to contact the ball as you would when hitting a forehand (see Figure 3.3). The racket should rotate between the forehand and the backhand like a windshield wiper. Notice that with the Seemiller grip your palm faces away from the body while with the shakehands grip, it faces toward the body. Remember to stroke the ball; don't just stick the racket out and block the ball. The stroke itself is almost identical to a shakehands backhand.

Figure 3.3   The Seemiller grip for backhand.

With the penhold grip, the backhand becomes more difficult. It's a very cramped stroke, at least for a beginner. (Advanced players can do the stroke quite smoothly, almost as well as the best shakehands players.) As with the Seemiller grip, the same surface is used for hitting both the backhand and the forehand. The stroke itself is rather simple (see Figure 3.4, a-c). It's the cramped nature of the stroke that makes it more difficult. Many penhold players don't really stroke the backhand; they block it. This is okay, as long as they develop the forehand and the footwork to use it. Other penholders take a full stroke and swing at the ball (especially those with the Korean grip).

SMASH

A smash is simply a very hard forehand or backhand. Use a longer backswing to generate more power. Use more wrist for backhand smashes, and throw your body into the shot on forehand smashes. Use a vigorous quick forearm snapping gesture from the elbow on all smashes. Contact the ball straight on with no spin (very flat), and sink the ball through the sponge to the wood. Follow through longer than normal.

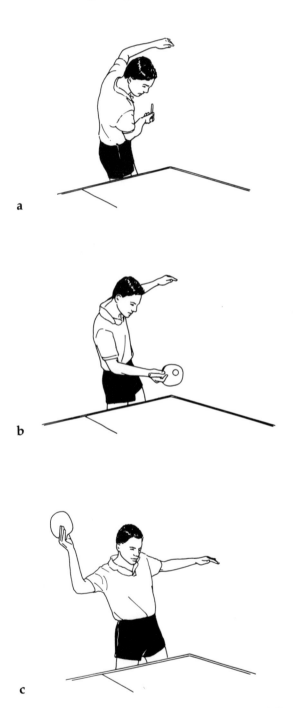

Figure 3.4   Backswing (a), forward swing (b), and follow-through (c) phases.

Detecting Forehand and Backhand Drive Errors

Some of the more common errors are shown below. Even advanced players make some of these mistakes, but there's no reason why you should!

ERROR   **CORRECTION**

ERROR	CORRECTION
1. The ball goes into the net or off the end.	1. Read the spin and adjust racket angle. If you're going into the net, aim higher and contact more under the ball. If you're going off the end, aim lower with a closed racket.
2. The shot feels strained or erratic.	2. Make sure you're executing each part of the forward swing in the correct sequence. On the forehand shot, the order should be weight transfer, hip and waist rotate, then forearm snap. On the backhand, the order should be forearm snap, then turn the top of wrist over so it faces the table. Make sure your muscles are relaxed.
3. No power.	3. Accelerate the racket into the ball more, using all parts of the stroke. Make sure you have a strong elbow snap. On the forehand, use more weight shift. On the backhand, increase the length of the backswing. Relax your muscles.
4. You're off balance during the shot.	4. Move to the ball, don't reach.

Forehand and Backhand Drive Drills

Whenever starting a forehand or backhand drive drill in this section, the server should serve topspin if he or she knows how. If not, the player should simply serve to get the ball in play, without putting any spin on the ball. Follow basic service rules given in the "Table Tennis Today" section on service rules. Make sure the ball hits both sides of the table when you serve.

1. Ready Stance

Get into a ready position. Make sure to stay relaxed. Imagine yourself about to hit a ball. You should feel like a coiled spring. Then relax (as if it were between points), and go into a ready stance again. This drill simulates a game situation where you would go into a good ready position at the start of each rally. Experiment with different ready stances until you find one that feels comfortable to use with both the forehand and backhand shots. Note that regardless of whether the stance favors one side, you should be equally ready to hit a forehand or a backhand with any stance. (Favoring one side means that your body is in a better position to hit on that side, not that you are expecting that shot.)

Success Goal = Go into your ready stance at least 10 times

Your Score = (#) _____ consecutive times into ready position

2. Forehand and Backhand Drives

Have your partner hit forehand crosscourt to your forehand. Return it with a forehand drive. Your partner should catch the ball and repeat. Repeat with backhand. Make sure to get in a ready position after each shot.

Success Goal = 20 consecutive forehand and 20 consecutive backhand returns

Your Score =

    (#) _____ consecutive forehand returns

    (#) _____ consecutive backhand returns

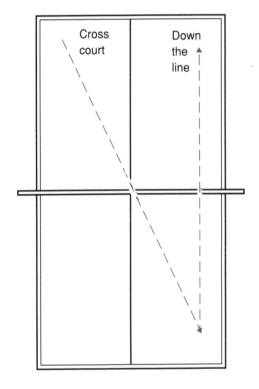

3. *Crosscourt Hitting*

Hit forehand to forehand, crosscourt, with a partner. Go slow at first until you find a good pace. Try to hit each ball exactly the same and to keep the ball in play. Do the same backhand to backhand. These are your first true rallying drills, and the most common way to warm up at the start of a playing session. Practicing these shots in this manner is the first step toward perfecting them in a game situation.

Success Goal = 20 consecutive forehands and 20 consecutive backhands

Your Score =

    (#) _____ consecutive forehands

    (#) _____ consecutive backhands

4. *Forehand and Backhand Down the Line*

This drill enables you and your partner to drive the ball down the line rather than always crosscourt. You hit forehand from the forehand corner down the line to your partner's backhand, who drives the ball backhand down the line to you. Make sure to contact the ball at the exact point opposite the direction you want the ball to go. For example, if you want the ball to go to the left, you should contact the ball on its right side. You will be hitting forehands down the line with topspin while your opponent does backhands down the line, and vice versa.

Success Goal = 20 consecutive forehands and 20 consecutive backhands down the line

Your Score =

    (#) _____ consecutive forehands down the line

    (#) _____ consecutive backhands down the line

5. *Smashing*

Hit forehand crosscourt to your partner, who returns the ball with a weak drive. Smash the return. Do the same with the backhand. (You might want to use a bucket of balls for this drill rather than keep picking up the ball.)

Success Goal = 10 consecutive smashes

Your Score =

    (#) _____ consecutive forehand smashes

    (#) _____ consecutive backhand smashes

6. *Random Drill*

Your partner backhand drives the ball to either your forehand or backhand side randomly. You drive each ball back with either forehand or backhand, depending on where your partner hits the ball. Continue to rally in this way for 15 consecutive drives. Your partner should drive the ball toward the corners, but not so wide as to make you move around too much. The purpose of this drill is to make a decision as to whether to use a forehand or a backhand shot. You'll have to move some to get to each shot, but that's not the focus of this drill. Make sure to get into a ready position after each shot, otherwise the drill will be nearly impossible. Be ready for shots on either side. Don't overanticipate where the next shot is going—wait until your partner is committed on direction before you react. This means waiting until your opponent contacts the ball or a split second before.

Success Goal = 15 consecutive shots, forehand or backhand

Your Score = (#) _____ consecutive forehands or backhands

7. *Backhand-Backhand Game*

Play a game with your partner, backhand to backhand drives only. Only shots that land on the backhand side of the table count—misses are a lost point. (If you both disagree as to whether shot was in, it is a "let"— take it over.) Play games to 11; you have to win by 2. Experiment: Are you more successful playing consistently or aggressively?

Success Goal = Win at least half of the games played

Your Score = (#) _____ wins, (#) _____ losses

Forehand and Backhand Drives Keys to Success Checklist

Have your instructor or practice partner critique your forehand and backhand drives with the Keys to Success checklist in Figure 3.2. Verify that you're ready to hit both forehand and backhand drives from your ready stance by having an observer critique your progress. Your observer should pay close attention to whether each part of the stroke is done in the proper order.

Step 4   Beginning Serves: Getting the Initiative

Before you play regulation games, you need to know how to put the ball in play—how to serve. There are four serves that you should learn right from the beginning: forehand topspin, backhand topspin, forehand backspin, and backhand backspin.

These serves are the foundation. Learn them and you'll be ready to develop serves that will really give your opponent problems!

WHY ARE THESE SERVES IMPORTANT?

You could just pat the ball high over the net when you serve, just to get it into play. But this would give your opponent an easy shot to start the rally off with. Since your opponent no doubt has spent many hours perfecting her serve, she'll be taking the initiative when she serves, and you'll be at a severe disadvantage if you can't do the same.

By taking some time to practice your own serves, you won't give your opponent a good ball to start the rally off with when you serve. If your opponent is strong against one serve, you'll have others to use instead. You'll get the first strong shot.

Topspin serves enable you to serve faster than other serves. They are favored by players who like to go for hard drives against topspin right from the start of the rally. Topspin serves can be done very fast to any part of the table, and the topspin will often force a high return. The risk, however, is that topspin serves are easier to attack than other serves. Topspin servers should be ready to hit or counter-hit right after the serve. Most players will return a topspin serve with a topspin drive of some sort.

Backspin serves are used to set up a heavy topspin attack. They're a safe way to serve, because backspin serves are difficult to attack, especially if they land short on the table. When serving backspin, you'll probably get a backspin return. Backspin servers usually attack with heavy topspin, because the likely backspin return can be attacked with heavy topspin very easily.

Don't just serve to put the ball in play: Serve with a plan. Try to use serves that will give you returns that you're comfortable with. For example, if you like to attack against backspin, serve heavy backspin, especially to your opponent's backhand

side, and you'll probably get a backspin push return—just what you wanted (explained in Step 6). If you like to drive the ball against topspin, serve topspin and you'll usually get a topspin return. If you aren't sure which type you like yet, learn both types of serves, and later on you'll find which type you favor.

If your opponent is weak against a certain serve or shot, play into it. If he has trouble returning serves to the forehand, you know where to serve. If she doesn't like topspin rallies, serve topspin. Remember—the server starts the rally, and he gets to choose what type of rally will start out.

In doubles, players serve from the right-hand court crosscourt to the opponent's right-hand court. In singles, however, you may serve from anywhere on your side of the table to anywhere on your opponent's side. However, you must contact the ball behind your endline when serving.

Before you learn to serve you have to know the service rules (see Figure 4.1). They are as follows (see the section on rules in "Table Tennis Today" for a more thorough treatment):

1. Ball in palm
2. Palm flat and stationary
3. Fingers together and thumb free
4. Racket and free hand above table
5. Racket and free hand behind endline
6. Toss ball six inches or more
7. No spin imparted by toss
8. Contact ball as it drops
9. Ball bounces once on each side of table

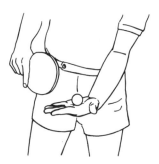

Figure 4.1   Beginning position for serving.

You also need to know some terminology. A *short* serve, if given the chance, bounces twice or more on the opponent's side of the table. A *long* serve only has the chance to bounce once on the opposite side of the table. A *crosscourt* serve goes diagonally from one corner to the other. A *down the line* serve travels from corner to corner on one of the two sidelines. These terms also apply to shots other than serves.

HOW TO EXECUTE A TOPSPIN SERVE

You can serve a topspin serve with either extreme topspin or extreme speed, depending on whether you hit the ball with a grazing motion or contact it straight on (flat). Learn both, because many players will have trouble with one but not the other.

For maximum spin, contact the ball with an upward grazing motion. For maximum speed, serve mostly crosscourt to give the ball more time to drop. Practice your serves both crosscourt and down the line, however.

Start by standing in position, usually toward your backhand side. For a forehand topspin serve, face slightly to the right; for a backhand topspin serve, face the table (see Figure 4.2a).

Pull your arm back and toss the ball up at the same time. For extra speed, pull the racket straight back; for extra topspin, pull it a little down (see Figure 4.2b). As the ball starts to drop, pull the racket forward at your elbow. Contact the ball low to the table, very flat for speed, with an upward grazing motion for extra topspin. At contact, snap your wrist—upward for spin, forward for speed (see Figure 4.2c). The racket should be perpendicular to the floor or slightly closed at contact. Follow through naturally, with your wrist turning over (see Figure 4.2d).

The ball should bounce first on your side of the table very near your endline. The second bounce should be near the opponent's endline—very deep. This gives the ball the most time to drop between bounces, letting you serve faster, because the major limit to speed on the serve is getting the ball to drop quickly enough to hit the other side. Serving so the ball lands near your opponent's endline also makes the opponent return the ball from as far away as possible from her target (your side of the table), making the serve more difficult to return effectively.

Make sure the ball crosses the net very low. If it goes high, you're hitting down on the ball too much at contact.

Figure 4.2   Keys to Success:
Topspin Serves

Preparation
Phase

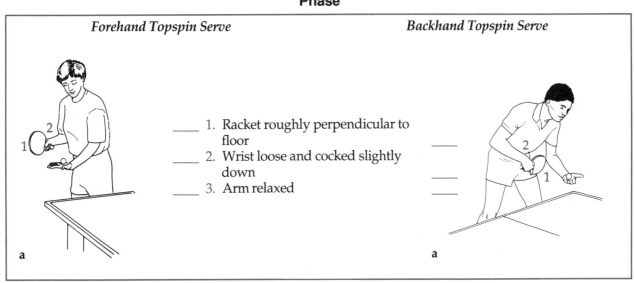

Forehand Topspin Serve

_____ 1. Racket roughly perpendicular to floor
_____ 2. Wrist loose and cocked slightly down
_____ 3. Arm relaxed

Backhand Topspin Serve

a

a

Execution
Phase

Backswing

Forehand Topspin Serve   *Backhand Topspin Serve*

_____ 1. Draw racket back roughly 1 foot
_____ 2. Toss ball upward between 6
         inches and eye level

b   b

Forward Swing

Forehand Topspin Serve   *Backhand Topspin Serve*

_____ 1. Racket moves forward
_____ 2. Graze the back of the ball upward
         for extra topspin
_____ 3. Contact the back of the ball very
         flat for extra speed

c   c

Follow-Through
Phase

Forehand Topspin Serve   *Backhand Topspin Serve*

_____   1. Follow through naturally
_____   2. Follow through slightly up for
           extra topspin
_____   3. Follow through straight forward
           for extra speed

_____

_____

_____

d   d

HOW TO EXECUTE A BACKSPIN SERVE

The backspin serve is similar to the topspin serve with these differences: Your racket should be open throughout the serve (see Figure 4.3a). Bring the racket slightly upward during the backswing, with your wrist cocked up (see Figure 4.3b). Then bring the racket down to the ball, contacting the back bottom of the ball (as much under as you can) with a grazing motion, snapping your wrist at contact (see Figure 4.3, c and d). The ball should travel slowly, because most of your racket speed causes backspin on the ball, not speed.

At first, your serves will probably go long. Serving with good backspin is more important than depth control at this point. However, if you can learn to serve a backspin serve so it goes short, it will be harder for your opponent to attack it. A short serve is one where the ball bounces twice on the opponent's side of the table. It is easier to serve backspin and no-spin short than other spins. To serve short make sure the first bounce (on your side of the table) is near the net. Contact the ball with a fine grazing motion so there isn't much forward motion and try to make the ball bounce twice on the other side (assuming your opponent doesn't hit it). However, don't sacrifice spin to keep the ball short. If you keep the bounce low (as you should for all serves), the ball will also go shorter. Serving crosscourt also gives more table room to keep the ball short.

Figure 4.3   Keys to Success: Backspin Serves

Preparation Phase

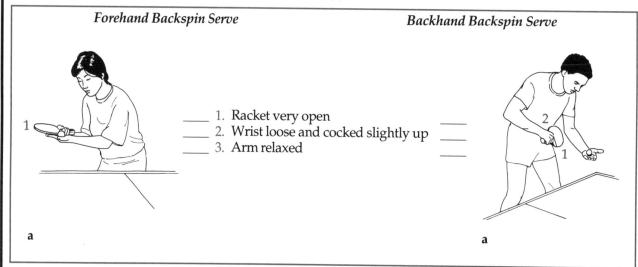

Forehand Backspin Serve   *Backhand Backspin Serve*

1

_____ 1. Racket very open   _____
_____ 2. Wrist loose and cocked slightly up   _____
_____ 3. Arm relaxed   _____

2

1

a   a

Execution Phase

Backswing

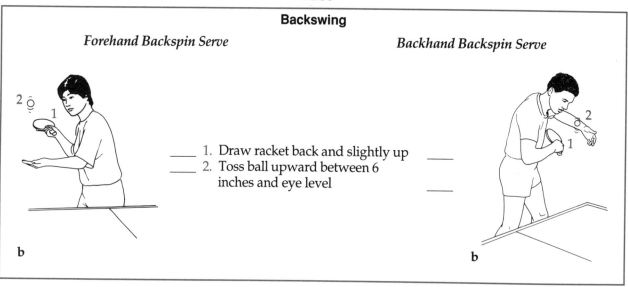

Forehand Backspin Serve   *Backhand Backspin Serve*

2   1

_____ 1. Draw racket back and slightly up   _____
_____ 2. Toss ball upward between 6   _____
       inches and eye level

2

1

b   b

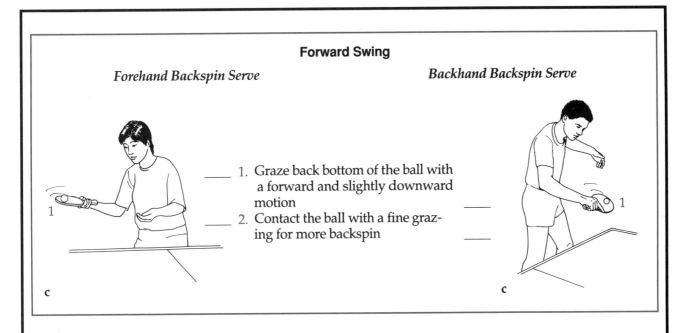

Forward Swing

Forehand Backspin Serve

Backhand Backspin Serve

_____ 1. Graze back bottom of the ball with a forward and slightly downward motion

_____ 2. Contact the ball with a fine grazing for more backspin

Follow-Through Phase

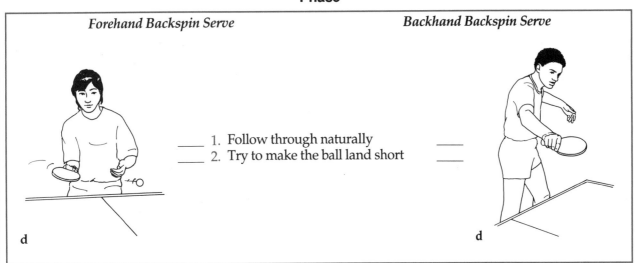

Forehand Backspin Serve

Backhand Backspin Serve

_____ 1. Follow through naturally
_____ 2. Try to make the ball land short

Detecting Topspin and Backspin Serve Errors

Even if you can't make great serves overnight, you can at least make good ones very quickly by following some basic principles. A few common errors account for most service problems, and addressing them will greatly enhance your serves.

ERROR 🚫

CORRECTION

1. Your serve bounces too high making it easy for your opponent to attack.

2. Your serve goes into the net.

3. Your serve goes off the table.

4. You miss the ball entirely.

5. You're not generating enough spin.

6. Your serves are erratic.

7. You can't keep your backspin serve short.

8. You can't hit the topspin serve fast enough.

1. Contact the ball lower and make sure not to hit downward at contact. This is the most common cause of a high bounce.

2. Make sure your first bounce isn't so close to the net that it can't rise.

3. Either you're serving too fast or your serve is bouncing too high. The ball doesn't have a chance to drop on the other side.

4. Keep your eye on the ball. Toss the ball slightly higher so you have more time to watch it and time your contact.

5. Make sure to graze the ball. Generate racket speed with loose muscles, longer backswing, and wrist.

6. Make sure the stroke and contact are the same each time. Make sure your arm is relaxed.

7. Graze the ball more. Make the first bounce near the net and very low.

8. Make sure your arm is loose. Snap your forearm and wrist into the shot and hit mostly forward.

HOW TO RETURN SERVES

At this point, your opponent (if he or she's learning from this book) has two main types of serves: topspin and backspin. You now need to know how to return them.

When your opponent serves topspin, use the forehand or backhand drives learned earlier. Place the ball so your opponent can't use his or her stronger side—if he or she's weak on the backhand, for example, that's where you should return most serves.

When your opponent serves backspin, you can also use the forehand and backhand drives. Remember to adjust for the backspin—it's a little more tricky than adjusting for topspin because you have to hit upward while still getting the ball to drop on the other side. Later on you'll learn other ways to return backspin serves, but it's important that you learn how to topspin drive them back first.

Beginning Service Drills

For the following drills, you'll need either a bucket of balls or a partner. Serious players always have a bucket of balls around to practice serves when they have no partner.

1. Topspin Serves

Serve forehand topspin serves. Do them from both the left and right sides of the table. Concentrate on serving with good topspin, as low as possible. Repeat with backhand topspin serves. Repeat the entire exercise, this time using fast topspin serves, emphasizing speed instead of spin. Serve mostly crosscourt (because it gives you more room to serve). This drill should give you both the ability and the confidence to perform all types of topspin serves—forehand, backhand, fast, and increased spin serves.

Success Goal = 30 consecutive forehand topspin serves and 30 consecutive backhand topspin serves emphasizing spin, then speed

Your Score =

(#) _____ consecutive forehand topspin serves

(#) _____ consecutive backhand topspin serves

(#) _____ consecutive fast forehand topspin serves

(#) _____ consecutive fast backhand topspin serves

2. Backspin Serves

Serve forehand backspin serves from both forehand and backhand sides of the table. Concentrate on getting good backspin and keeping the ball low. Repeat with backhand backspin serves. This drill should help you learn how to perform forehand and backhand backspin serves to all parts of the table with confidence.

Success Goal = 30 consecutive forehand backspin serves and 30 consecutive backhand backspin serves

Your Score =

(#) _____ consecutive forehand backspin serves

(#) _____ consecutive backhand backspin serves

3. Service Accuracy

Put a small target on the table, such as the lid to a jar or a broken ball. Try to hit it with one of the serves you've learned. Put the target a few inches from the far corner of the table for topspin serves, somewhere in the middle of the table for backspin serves. Do this with forehand and backhand topspin and backspin serves. This drill will teach you accuracy so that you can serve the ball where you want to.

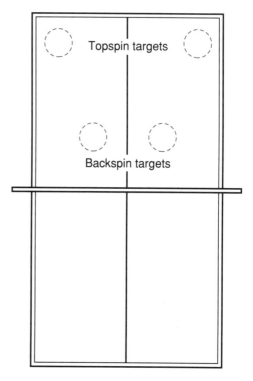

Success Goal = Hit the target 5 times with all four types of serves

Your Score =

(#) _____ hit targets with forehand topspin
serve

(#) _____ hit targets with backhand topspin
serve

(#) _____ hit targets with forehand backspin
serve

(#) _____ hit targets with backhand backspin
serve

4. Side to Side Accuracy

Play an accuracy game. Put four targets on the table, one near each far corner, one in the middle backhand area, one in the middle forehand area. Serve two consecutive topspin serves deep (that is, the ball should bounce near your opponent's endline), aiming for the corner targets, then two consecutive backspin serves, aiming for the two closer targets. Do this in a circuit. See who can hit the most targets in the circuit in a given amount of repetitions. Use both forehand and backhand serves.

Success Goal = Hit more targets than your partner at least once

Your Score = (#) _____ targets hit in 1 circuit

5. *Short Backspin*

Serve a backspin serve short. The ball should bounce twice on the other side of the table. Make sure to graze the ball so it will travel slowly; make sure the first bounce on your side is near the net. You might have a contest to see who can make the most short serves in a given amount of time. Review Figure 4.3a-d to hit a successful short backspin serve.

Success Goal = 10 short forehand backspin serves and 10 short backhand backspin serves

Your Score =
   (#) _____ short forehand backspin serves
   (#) _____ short backhand backspin serves

6. *Service Accuracy Game*

Put several paper cups or similar light objects at the edge of your side and your opponent's side of the table. Each player takes turns serving the ball, trying to knock a cup off the table. Whoever knocks off all the cups first wins. (You can continue rallying after the serve.) Try to use the different serves you have learned in this step for each turn.

Success Goal = Knock off all the cups first at least once

Your Score = (#) _____ times knocked all the cups off first

7. *Backhand-Forehand Game*

Play an 11-point game with these rules: Server always serves backspin forehand or backhand to partner's backhand. Partner returns with a backhand drive to server's backhand. Rally continues, backhand to backhand, until one player suddenly goes down the line to the opponent's forehand. Whoever gets the forehand shot has to smash; then it's open play until the point is won (if the smash is returned).

Success Goal = Win at least 1 game with these rules

Your Score = (#) _____ times won

8. *Topspin Serve and Attack Game*

Play to 11 points. Serve topspin to any part of your partner's side of the table. Your partner drives it back with a forehand or backhand drive, and you attack (hit harder) with forehand or backhand drives. In this game, the server has to be the aggressor, trying to end the point as quickly as possible, while the receiver plays consistent drives. Then repeat, serving backspin, with your partner returning with a forehand or backhand drive. (If your partner knows how to do backspin returns—pushing—your partner can push, and you can make the first topspin drive.)

Success Goal = Win at least 1 game at topspin serve and attack and at least 1 game at backspin serve and attack

Your Score =

(#) _____ times won at topspin serve and attack

(#) _____ times won at backspin serve and attack

Beginning Serves
Keys to Success Checklists

Have your instructor or practice partner observe your serves and verify that they are being done properly, using the Keys to Success checklists (see Figures 4.2 and 4.3). Have them observe that you are doing all four major serves correctly—forehand and backhand topspin and backspin serves. They should verify that you're getting good spin on all four serves, and figure out why if you're not. Pay particular attention to the contact on each serve—make sure you're grazing the ball and accelerating into the serve, not just going through the motion.

Step 5   Positioning and Footwork: How to Move to the Ball

How you position yourself at the table often sets the tone for your future efforts. If you position yourself correctly, you'll tend to play correctly. If you don't, you cannot possibly play correctly. You'll have to learn the correct methods to move into position and execute any necessary shot if you wish to improve. In this step you will first learn correct positioning, then correct footwork using the two-step method.

Positioning is where you stand. Footwork is how you get into position. Without good footwork, you won't be in position for most shots.

WHY POSITIONING AND FOOTWORK ARE IMPORTANT

You can't return a ball if you're 5 feet away as it whizzes by! The better your positioning is, the less distance you'll have to cover when moving to a shot and the less rushed the shot will be. You have to be able to put yourself in a position that allows you to get to any shot made by your opponent.

Some players stand in one area and just reach for each shot. This means that they hit a ball from their middle forehand, wide forehand, and close to the body forehand differently, as well as all shots in between. The same goes for the backhand. It's impossible to learn to hit all these different types of forehands and backhands as well as you could learn to hit just one type of forehand and one type of backhand. Reaching instead of moving means you'll always be off balance when you hit the ball.

POSITIONING

Many players automatically position themselves in the middle of the table. This is incorrect. Your ready stance should be somewhat to the left of the centerline (see Figure 5.1). (Note that this is for right-handers. Here, and elsewhere in the book, left-handers reverse.)

Three things must be considered when you position yourself; they must be done automatically:

- The playing elbow marks the midpoint between the forehand and the backhand, so you should keep your playing elbow near the center of the table. This moves your whole body to

the left. (When a player hits to the "middle," he isn't hitting to the middle of the table—he's hitting to the opponent's middle. This is defined to be his playing elbow, which is in the middle of his forehand and backhand contact points.)

- Many players have a stronger forehand than backhand and should therefore favor it whenever possible. (Note that if a player has a stronger backhand than forehand, she probably should not use it from the forehand court—the backhand has limited range.) If a player does favor the forehand, she should intentionally stand as far to the left as possible, covering as much ground as possible with the forehand. A good rule for a forehand-oriented player is to stand as far to the left as possible and still be able to just cover the wide forehand corner effectively.

- Your opponent's position has to be taken into account. For example, if your opponent moves to the left, you have to move to the right to cover the angle to your right.

Figure 5.1   Correct positioning.

Many players have difficulty with a ball hit at their playing elbow, their middle, because they have to make a quick decision on whether to use the forehand or backhand. A general rule to follow is if the ball is hit to your middle, it's usually best to use a backhand to return hard-hit shots if you're close to the table. Use the forehand against weaker shots or when you're away from the table.

You should start every rally in the ready stance. Between shots, even if you're way out of position, you should be in your ready stance as the opponent hits the ball.

FOOTWORK

The table is only 5 feet wide, which doesn't seem like much. But when the ball starts traveling at speeds close to 100 miles per hour (and long before it gets that fast) you'll have to know how to get into position for each shot.

The key is to move into a position that allows you to hit any given shot at the same point in relation to the body. For example, good players will always make contact on their forehand at about 2 feet to the side (depending on the length of their arm), but whatever distance it is, they'll always hit at that distance.

Sometimes you will be close but not quite in position. Don't be lazy—move. You want to be in perfect position for every shot. If the move is very small, you can make it by moving only one leg, especially with the backhand. For example, if the ball is to your wide backhand and you don't have much time, take a short step with your left leg to get into position. But if you have time, it's better to move both feet, using the methods shown in this chapter.

There are many styles of footwork. Some should be used only by players who favor that one style. Some styles are more general and should be mastered by all players. Rather than cover all types, I'll cover the most popular and successful method of footwork. However, there are a few fundamentals of all footwork. First, always keep your weight on the balls of your feet. Second, be bouncy. Many top players even bounce slightly on their feet between shots. It keeps you primed to move. Third, always move left or right the instant after the other player is committed to his shot, but never before.

The type of footwork I'll teach is called *two-step footwork*; it's used mostly for moving side to side.

Two-Step Footwork

This is the most popular method of footwork; it's used by nearly all top level attackers. It's quick and covers a lot of ground.

Two-step footwork is used in moving sideways in either direction. You can use it to cover the wide forehand with the forehand, the forehand out of the backhand corner, and to cover the wide backhand with the backhand. A version of it is also used to move to and away from the table.

Get into your ready position (see Figure 5.2a). Let's say you're moving to the left.

Start by taking a short step, about 4 to 6 inches long, with the left leg (see Figure 5.2b). This puts your legs farther apart and starts your momentum. Pull with the left leg, letting your weight transfer onto it. Move both feet to the left. Use the momentum from the short shuffle step to pull your body to the left. Both feet should move, coming closer together in the middle of the motion (see Figure 5.2c) but ending up with your feet the same distance apart as at the start of the motion (see Figure 5.2d). Your right foot should end up about where the left foot was after the short step.

To move to the right, use the same motion except switch left and right. If you're moving into position to hit a forehand, you should pull your right leg back slightly so as to be in a proper forehand position when you arrive.

Suppose you're too far away from the table to make a good shot. You can use two-step footwork to get closer to the table. If you want to hit a forehand, move as if you were going to the left except move your left leg forward, following with your right leg. If you're going to hit a backhand, lead with your right foot. For all in and out motions, lead with the foot that puts you in the best position for the stroke. If you have to cover more ground than one application of two-step footwork would allow, run.

Sometimes you'll need to cover a lot of ground (side to side) in a hurry, especially after hitting a forehand from the backhand corner. You have to be able to cover that almost inevitable quick block to the wide forehand. You can use two-step footwork to do so, but to cover the extra ground you may have to do two-step footwork twice in succession, without the short step on the second one.

Figure 5.2   **Keys to Success:**
Two-Step Footwork
(Moving to the left—reverse left and right to move to the right)

**Preparation
Phase**

1. Knees slightly bent ____
2. Weight evenly distributed between both legs ____
3. Weight on inside balls of the feet ____

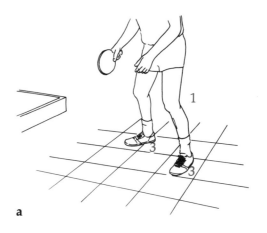

a

**Execution
Phase**

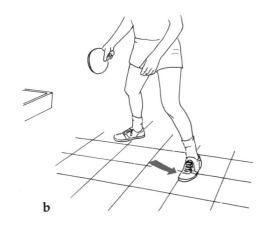

b

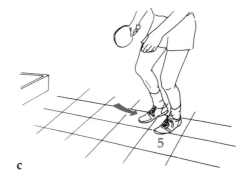

c

1. Left foot takes a short step ____
2. Weight begins to shift to left ____
3. Left leg pulls ____

4. Both feet shuffle to left ____
5. Feet come together in middle of motion ____

Follow-Through
Phase

1. Left leg moves to the left ____
2. If preparing for forehand, right leg pulls back slightly ____
3. End in position for stroke ____
4. Start backswing stroke immediately after footwork ____

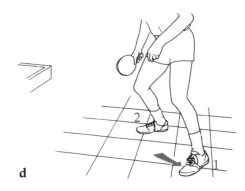

d

GETTING BACK INTO POSITION

After hitting any shot, don't stand around admiring it. It just might come back! Always expect it to. You have to get back into position.

To do so, push with your right leg to go left, your left leg to go right. If you're way out of position, get back as far as you can, but never be in motion when the opponent hits the ball. It's better to be ready to cover most of the court and hope she doesn't hit a strong shot to the part you can't cover. If you're in motion, you won't be able to effectively cover the part you're moving away from, and even a weak shot there will give you trouble.

Detecting Footwork Errors

Many players with seemingly poor strokes actually suffer from footwork problems. Poor footwork can make anybody's shots look poor; good footwork will carry poor strokes a long way. Footwork is the most tiring part of the game to practice, but top players consider it the most important practice of all. Even a player with slow feet can improve immensely by using correct footwork and avoiding some of the more common errors.

ERROR 🚫

CORRECTION

1. Your feet bounce too high or lift off the ground.

2. You're not in position at the end of the movement.

1. Your feet should stay low to the ground, almost sliding.

2. Make adjustments during and after the movement.

ERROR	**CORRECTION**
3. Your heels are on the ground.	3. Your weight should be on the inside balls of your feet.
4. You're reaching for the ball.	4. Try not to reach for the ball, but instead use the two-step footwork. Move the leg that is in the direction you want to go and follow up with the other leg.

Positioning and Footwork Drills

1. Positioning and Shot Selection

Write down the answers to the following:

    a. When your opponent moves to the left, which side of the table do you cover?
    b. If your opponent moves to the right, which side of the table do you cover?
    c. When a player hits the ball to your middle (your playing elbow), when would you use your forehand?
    d. When a player hits a ball to your middle, when would you use your backhand?

Success Goal = Respond to the questions

Your Score = Answers to the questions

    a. If your opponent moves left, you cover the _____ side

    b. If your opponent moves right, you cover the _____ side

    c. Use forehand: _____

    _____

    d. Use backhand: _____

    _____

2. Two-Step Footwork Practice

Practice moving side to side with two-step footwork. Start slow and build up speed. Keep your feet low to the ground. If you do this by a table, touch the right corner with your left hand when you move right; touch the left corner with your right hand when you move left. Do this drill to help you monitor how far you need to move in each direction. This will also develop two-step agility.

Success Goal = Side to side 50 times correctly

Your Score = (#) _____ correct repetitions

3. One-One Footwork Drill

Have your partner hit forehands side to side, alternating one to your wide forehand, one to the middle of the table. Return them all with your forehand, using two-step footwork. As you get better, try covering two-thirds of the table.

Success Goal = 20 consecutive repetitions of one-one footwork drill

Your Score = (#) _____ consecutive repetitions of one-one footwork drill

4. Figure Eight

One player hits everything crosscourt, alternating forehands and backhands. The other player hits everything down the line, also alternating forehands and backhands. The ball travels in a figure eight. Players move side to side for each shot, using two-step footwork. Then repeat, with each player reversing roles.

Success Goal = 20 consecutive shots, both crosscourt and down the line using two-step footwork

Your Score =
  (#) _____ crosscourt figure eight shots using two-step footwork
  (#) _____ down the line figure eight shots using two-step footwork

5. Forehand/Backhand Footwork

Have your partner hit backhands to your backhand corner, crosscourt. You alternate forehand and backhand drives from backhand corner, moving side to side with two-step footwork.

Success Goal = 20 consecutive repetitions of forehand/backhand footwork

Your Score = (#) _____ consecutive repetitions of forehand/backhand footwork

6. Two-One Footwork Drill

Your partner hits only backhand drives, two to your backhand side, one to your forehand side, over and over. You hit a backhand from your backhand corner, then use two-step footwork to step around and hit a forehand drive from the backhand side. Then you use two-step footwork to cover a wide forehand with your forehand. Then use two-step footwork to get back into position to hit a backhand drive from your backhand corner. Rally continues.

Success Goal = 15 consecutive rounds of two-one footwork drill

Your Score = (#) _____ consecutive rounds of two-one footwork drill

7. Figure Eight Game

Play games, using the figure eight path described in Drill 4. One player hits everything crosscourt, the other down the line. If a player hits to the wrong side, it's a lost point. The middle line tells whether the ball is hit on the correct side or not. Play best-of-three games to 21 points (a match), with each player hitting crosscourt one game, down the line one game, and trading roles as soon as a player reaches 10 points in the third game.

Success Goal = Win at least 1 best-of-3-games match

Your Score = (#) _____ matches won

8. Two-Step Footwork Race

Set up two tables side by side, about 7 feet apart (closer if players are short). Fill two buckets with an equal amount of balls; put them on one table on opposite sides near the endlines. Put two empty buckets on opposite sides of the other table. Players use two-step footwork and go back and forth, picking up the balls in the full bucket and putting them in the empty bucket. Players can only handle the balls with their playing hands. Two or more can race each other in this game (you need more buckets and possibly more tables if more than two race at one time). Whoever moves all the balls from one bucket to the other first wins.

Success Goal = Move all the balls from one bucket to the other first

Your Score = (#) _____ times moved all the balls from one bucket to the other first

Positioning and Footwork Keys to Success Checklist

The importance of footwork in table tennis cannot be overemphasized. The difference between hitting a ball while in position, and trying to do so while reaching, is the difference between a successful and an unsuccessful player. Discuss with your instructor, coach, or practice partner the proper positioning for different circumstances, especially pertaining to how your opponent's position affects yours. Then have your partner or coach observe your two-step footwork and make sure it's being done properly, using the Keys to Success checklist (see Figure 5.2). Pay particular attention to staying balanced, knees slightly bent, and doing each step in a smooth progression. Make sure you're ready to start your stroke as soon as you get into position.

Answers to Drill 1

a. Cover the right side.

b. Cover the left side.

c. Usually use your forehand if the ball is hit softly or if you are far away from the table.

d. Usually use your backhand if the ball is hit hard and you are close to the table.

Step 6   Pushing: Your Basic Backspin Shot

The push is a passive backspin shot done against backspin. It's generally done against a backspin serve or push that you don't feel comfortable attacking, either for tactical reasons or because pushing is a more consistent way of returning backspin. The trick is to push so your opponent can't attack effectively. Keep the ball low, place it well, and give it a good backspin.

First I'll cover the basic push with a variation included for the Seemiller grip, then the more advanced pushes: the spin push, fast push, and short push.

WHY IS THE PUSH IMPORTANT?

The simplest way to return a ball with backspin is with a backspin push. The push is valuable for returning backspin serves or for returning backspin balls that you aren't ready to attack. A push can be attacked, but a good push can make that attack difficult.

HOW TO EXECUTE THE PUSH

Face the table (see Figure 6.1a). Rotate your upper body slightly to the right for a forehand push. Face the table directly for a backhand push. Point your elbow forward, away from your body; open your racket and bring it back and slightly up, pivoting at the elbow. Your elbow shouldn't move much during the stroke. Cock your wrist back (see Figure 6.1b).

Rotate the racket forward and slightly down. Let the ball fall onto the racket, grazing the bottom back of the ball to create backspin (see Figure 6.1c). Snap your wrist forward and slightly down at contact.

Follow through by straightening your arm until it's almost fully extended (see Figure 6.1d). Return to ready position.

Figure 6.1   Keys to Success: Forehand and Backhand Pushes

Preparation Phase

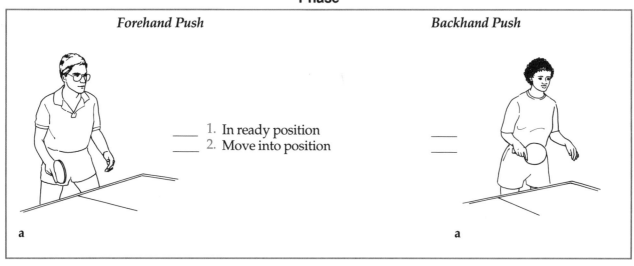

Forehand Push

_____ 1. In ready position
_____ 2. Move into position

Backhand Push

a

a

Execution
Phase

Backswing

Forehand Push   *Backhand Push*

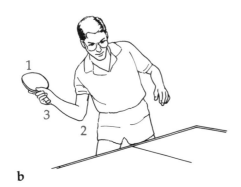

b

b

_____ 1. Open racket   _____
_____ 2. Bring arm backward and slightly   _____
       up, pivoting at elbow
_____ 3. Cock wrist back   _____

Forward Swing

Forehand Push   *Backhand Push*

_____ 1. Move racket forward from elbow   _____
_____ 2. Snap wrist at contact   _____

c

c

3. Contact the ball in front and   3. Contact the ball directly in
   slightly to the right of your   front of your body _____
   body _____

_____ 4. Graze back bottom of ball   _____

Follow-Through
Phase

| *Forehand Push* | *Backhand Push* |

_____ 1. Follow through forward and downward
_____ 2. Return to ready position

d

d

SEEMILLER GRIP PUSH

With the Seemiller grip you'll have to vary your grip for the backhand push, because it's awkward to open the racket on that side. Many players who use this grip bring their thumb around to the nonhitting side of the racket to open it (see Figure 6.2).

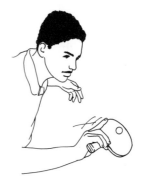

Figure 6.2 The Seemiller grip push.

Detecting Forehand and Backhand Push Errors

Pushing is a control shot; the most common mistake for beginners is to be too aggressive. Until you reach an advanced level, make the ball travel slowly when you push. Concentrate on consistency, placement, and spin.

ERROR

CORRECTION

1. The ball goes into the net or off the end, or pops up.

2. You're not getting enough backspin.

3. You don't have control of the ball.

1. Read the spin and adjust the racket angle.

2. Graze the ball more at contact. Contact more under the ball; use your wrist.

3. Make sure your stroke is smooth, not jerky. The push is a slow control shot, so don't stroke too fast. The aim is to keep the ball low with good backspin. Make sure you're moving to the ball, not reaching.

ADVANCED PUSHES

Advanced pushes can help you get an edge over your opponent. Top players use three types of pushes. The spin push (and its no-spin variation) is used against an opponent who has trouble with heavy backspin. The fast push gives an opponent less time to attack. A short push can be used to stop an opponent's attack.

Spin Push

A spin push is the same as a basic push except that the backspin is more severe. The purpose of a spin push is to either force an opponent into an error due to the heavy backspin, or to make your opponent hesitate to attack the push because of the heavy backspin, often allowing you to attack instead. To produce a spin push, take the ball as it drops and just graze it, using a lot of wrist. Contact the very bottom of the ball with a wide open racket. The ball should not travel fast—racket speed must be converted into spin. Keep the ball low and deep and many opponents won't be able to attack it effectively.

A variation of the spin push is the no-spin push, where you fake heavy backspin but give very little. There are two ways to achieve this. The first way is to contact the ball near the handle, since this part of the paddle moves slower than the rest of the hitting surface. (The tip, the farthest point from your wrist, moves fastest.) Even if you graze the ball, the ball will have less spin. If the opponent sees the grazing motion, your opponent may think there is more spin on the ball than there is. The other method is to fake a grazing motion but just pat the ball over instead,

hitting it straight on softly. Follow through vigorously to fake heavy spin.

Fast Push

This is a very fast, off the bounce push. It's used to keep an opponent from having time to attack effectively. It can be done with almost as much backspin as the spin push and is the most common deep push at the high levels of table tennis.

Contact the ball right off the bounce and push the racket forward quickly. The idea here is to push as quickly as possible. Push mostly to the backhand to keep your opponent from attacking with the forehand. Because there is backspin on the ball, if you push too fast the ball will go off the end. Nevertheless, if done properly, an opponent will have a hard time getting into position to attack with the forehand, and even a backhand attack will be rushed.

Short Push

At the highest levels of the game, may serves and returns are short. This is because any ball that is returned deep (where the ball goes past the table's endline after the first bounce) can be attacked easily. At the lower levels, this isn't as important, but as you advance, you'll want to be able to push short both to stop an opponent's attack and as a drop shot against defensive players. A ball that lands short on the table is difficult to attack because the table is in the way, while a push that lands deeper allows an opponent to take a full backswing.

Drop shots (a very short shot where the ball is just tapped over the net) against defensive players who back off the table too much should land as short on the table as possible, but other short pushes should usually go a little deeper, so that the second bounce on the far side of the table is near the endline. This makes it difficult for the opponent to attack effectively.

Take the ball right off the bounce with a soft touch. The racket should open slightly at contact, so start with the racket slightly more closed than you want. The stroke should be mostly downward with a slightly open racket. If your racket is too open, you'll pop the ball up. Because you're taking the ball on the rise, when it hits your racket it will bounce up, so you have to aim relatively low.

At first, you should just try to keep the ball low and short. With practice, you'll learn to do so with some backspin on the ball. Pushing short is a tricky shot, and at first you'll either go long or pop the ball up. You'll improve as your "touch" gets better.

If you're short and have trouble reaching a short push to the forehand side, you'll need to learn to step in for this shot. See Step 9 for a description of flipping (returning short balls) and stepping-in footwork.

Pushing Drills

Note: For all pushing drills, start with a backspin serve.

1. Crosscourt and Down the Line Pushing

You and your partner push backhand to backhand crosscourt, then forehand to forehand crosscourt, then forehand to backhand, down the line, and down both lines. Try to keep the ball low and with a good backspin. Don't try to load up the spin too much, however. The ball should travel slowly—this is not a speed shot. This drill teaches you to push to either side against any type of push.

Success Goal = 25 consecutive backhand and forehand pushes, both crosscourt and down the line

Your Score =

    (#) _____ consecutive crosscourt backhand pushes

    (#) _____ consecutive crosscourt forehand pushes

    (#) _____ consecutive down the line backhand pushes

    (#) _____ consecutive down the line forehand pushes

2. Random Pushing

You and your partner push anywhere. Try to keep the ball low and with a good backspin. Mix up your placement as much as possible; try not to let your partner know where your next push is going. This drill simulates a game situation, so you can learn to return with a push even if you don't know where the next shot will be.

Success Goal = 30 consecutive pushes done randomly with either the forehand or the backhand

Your Score = (#) _____ consecutive pushes, randomly with either forehand or backhand

3. Spin Push

Push backhand to backhand, practicing spin pushes. Concentrate on getting good backspin. Then do the same with the forehand. This drill gives you the skill to put extra backspin on the ball. You will have an obvious advantage if you master this skill and your opponent is weak against heavy backspin.

Success Goal = 20 consecutive backhand and 20 consecutive forehand spin pushes

Your Score =

   (#) _____ consecutive backhand spin pushes
   (#) _____ consecutive forehand spin pushes

4. Fast Push

Fast push backhand to backhand as many times as you can. Concentrate on pushing as quick off the bounce as possible. Then do the same with the forehand. This drill teaches you to push fast against a slow opponent.

Success Goal = 20 consecutive backhand and 20 consecutive forehand fast pushes

Your Score =

   (#) _____ consecutive backhand fast pushes
   (#) _____ consecutive forehand fast pushes

5. Short Push

Push short backhand to backhand as many times as you can. Concentrate on keeping the ball short and low but still with a little backspin. Then do the same with the forehand. Have your partner let some of your pushes go by so that you can see if they bounce twice or not. This drill teaches you how to use the length of the table against your opponent. You can stop an attack by pushing the ball so short your opponent has to reach over the table.

Success Goal = 15 consecutive backhand and 15 consecutive forehand short pushes

Your Score =

(#) _____ consecutive backhand short pushes

(#) _____ consecutive forehand short pushes

6. *Pushing Footwork*

Have your partner push backhands side to side, one to the left and one to the right. You push them back, alternating forehand and backhand and using two-step footwork. This drill gets you in the habit of moving to each ball rather than reaching for it. It also increases ball control.

Success Goal = 20 consecutive repetitions of two-step footwork combined with push

Your Score = (#) _____ consecutive repetitions of two-step footwork combined with pushes

7. *Random Pushing Game*

Play games to 11 points, push only. Use all types of pushes. For example, use long, short, fast, or spin pushes in varying sequences. This adds an element of surprise to your game while you try to force your opponent into error.

Success Goal = Win at least half of the games played

Your Score = (#) _____ games won, (#) _____ games lost

8. *Serve and Attack Against Backspin*

You serve backspin. Partner pushes to your backhand. You attack with your backhand drive and play out the point. Next, do the same sequence, but this time use two-step footwork and step around your backhand corner, attacking the push with your forehand drive from the backhand corner.

Success Goal = 20 points scored after attacking a push with a backhand drive, and 20 points scored after attacking a push with a forehand drive from backhand corner

Your Score =

(#) _____ points scored after attacking push with backhand drive

(#) _____ points scored after attacking push with forehand drive from backhand corner

9. *Random Attack Against Push*

You and your partner push all over the table, using all types of pushes. Try to force a weak or high push return. When you get one, attack with either forehand or backhand drive. If you can, smash. This drill teaches you to judge which ball to attack. Be patient; wait for the right ball to attack.

Success Goal = 20 points scored after attacking a push with either a forehand or backhand drive

Your Score = (#) _____ points scored after attacking a push with either a forehand or backhand drive

10. *Attacking Backspin Game*

Play a game with the following rules. Server always serves backspin. Receiver pushes it back to spot specified by server (usually backhand corner). Server attacks, either with forehand or backhand drive. Attack with forehand from forehand side of table; attack with forehand or backhand from backhand side of table. Games are to 11 points. This drill helps you incorporate attacking backspin into your game.

Success Goal = Win at least half of the games played

Your Score = (#) _____ games won, (#) _____ games lost

Pushing
Keys to Success Checklist

For you to be a proficient player, it is critical you master the various types of pushes. In this step you have learned both beginning and advanced pushes. Knowing the pushes will make it difficult for your opponent to attack effectively. Have your instructor or practice partner use the Keys to Success checklist (see Figure 6.1) to make sure you're doing the push stroke correctly. Then, practice Drill 7, the Random Pushing Game, to help you learn the short, long, heavy backspin, and fast pushes. Pay particular attention to using the wrist properly and grazing the ball. Ask your partner to critique your pushes, and use his or her comments as a way to improve.

Step 7   Blocking: Close-to-the-Table Defense

A block is a simple way of returning a hard drive. It is simpler than a drive, and many coaches teach it first for that reason. However, I prefer to teach it after a player has learned the drive because a drive is usually more effective against topspin than a block. A block should be used when an opponent's strong drive makes a drive return risky. Remember that a drive is an aggressive shot while a block is a more defensive return of a strong drive.

A block can be done either forehand or backhand. The stroke is similar to a drive except that there is no backswing and very little follow-through. There is also no weight shift. A block is best described as just that—a block. Just stick the racket in the way of a hard-hit ball. If the racket angle and contact are correct, the ball will go back low and fast.

Another difference between the block and the drive is that you should contact the ball earlier in a block. Take it right off the bounce. The block is most effective as a way to return an opponent's drive as quickly as possible so as not to give your opponent a chance to keep attacking.

In many of the drills you have done so far, both players used forehand or backhand drives in accomplishing the drill. However, as the pace of the rallies gets faster and faster (as you and your partner get better and better), it often becomes necessary for one player to drive, while the other blocks. At the higher levels, usually one player will block while the other player does a driving or footwork drill.

WHY IS THE BLOCK IMPORTANT?

Whenever possible, you want to use aggressive shots in table tennis (unless you're a defensive player). However, even an attacker is often faced with an opponent's attack, and if your opponent makes a strong enough attack, you won't be able to counterattack with your own drive. You'll have to block the ball. You just don't have time to do anything else.

This doesn't mean you're in trouble. Quick and well-placed blocks will win you many points. For example, if a player plays a forehand drive from the backhand side of the table, a quick block to the wide forehand will often win the point. In general, the goal is to return the ball so quickly, and so well-placed, that your opponent can't react or move quickly enough to continue the attack.

HOW TO EXECUTE THE BLOCK

Move into position—don't reach except as a final adjustment (see Figure 7.1). There should be no backswing. Just get the racket into position so that the incoming ball will contact it. To block successfully, use your opponent's speed and spin to return the ball. Contact should be made right after the bounce. Quickness is the important factor—you don't want to give your opponent time to make another strong shot. Hold the racket with a relaxed grip and let the ball sink into the sponge and trampoline back, usually with a light topspin. Try to contact the ball with the very center of the racket. At contact, move the racket forward a little, more so against a slow ball than against a fast one. Contact should be on the back of the ball, or slightly above. The quicker off the bounce you take the ball, the less you have to close your racket. Against heavy topspin, make sure to close the racket.

Follow-through should be short. Just move the racket forward naturally. Return to ready position. When blocking, you won't have time to execute two-step footwork. Instead, step directly toward the ball with your nearest foot.

One common variation of the block is the chop block. A chop block is just like a regular block except that at contact, you chop down on the ball to put some backspin on it. The chop block is a soft-touch shot, so hit the ball slowly. It's used both as a change of pace in a rally and as a return against a topspin serve.

Figure 7.1   Keys to Success:
   Forehand and Backhand Blocks

Preparation
Phase

Forehand Block   *Backhand Block*

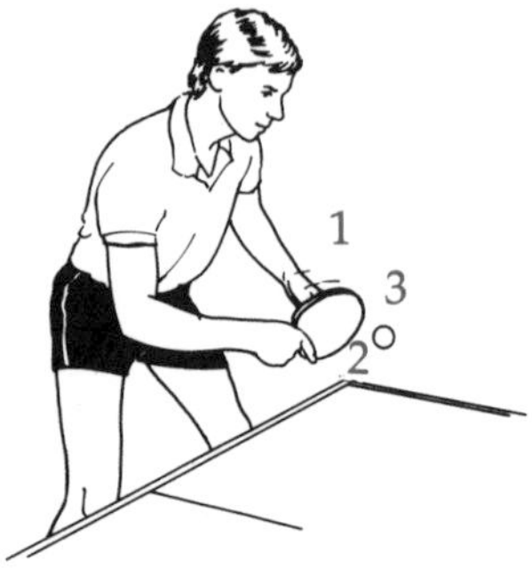

____ 1. Move into position   ____
____ 2. Close racket against heavy topspin   ____
____ 3. Racket tip slightly up   ____

Execution
Phase

Forehand Block   *Backhand Block*

____ 1. Contact quick off bounce   ____
____ 2. Contact very flat   ____
____ 3. Contact in center of racket   ____

Follow-Through
Phase

Forehand Block   *Backhand Block*

____ 1. Very short follow-through   ____

Detecting Forehand and Backhand Block Errors

More than any other shot, the block is a simple stroke. Follow the guidelines in Figure 7.1, watch out for the following errors, and your technique will improve. From then on, it's just a matter of timing, reflex, racket angle, and proper contact.

ERROR

CORRECTION

ERROR	CORRECTION
1. The ball goes into the net or off the end.	1. Read the spin and adjust your racket angle.
2. You're taking the ball too late so that your opponent has plenty of time to plan the next shot.	2. Stay close to the table and move to the ball—don't wait for it to come to you.
3. You're off balance.	3. Move to the ball. Don't reach.
4. You're inconsistent, with shots going off the end or into the net.	4. Keep your eye on the ball, and let the ball hit the center of the racket. Hold the racket with a relaxed grip and contact the ball at the center of the racket so that it sinks straight into the sponge, then trampolines back.

Blocking Drills

Note: Unless otherwise specified, players should always start rallies by serving topspin when doing blocking drills. Also note that although players need to be able to block on both the forehand and the backhand, it is more important to develop a very good backhand block, because it's easier to counterattack with your forehand.

1. Backhand and Forehand Blocks

Have your partner attack with either a forehand or backhand drive into your backhand. Your partner should hit relatively hard but not smash. Block the drive with your backhand. Try to contact the ball as quick off the bounce as possible. Then do the same with your forehand block. This is similar to the types of rallies you'll face in a match situation, where one player is attacking while the other is fending off the attack by blocking.

Success Goal = 20 consecutive backhand and 20 consecutive forehand blocks

Your Score =

(#) _____ consecutive backhand blocks

(#) _____ consecutive forehand blocks

2. *Blocking Side to Side*

Block to the forehand and backhand sides of the table with your backhand, one to the right, one to the left. Your partner attacks each ball into your backhand with either a forehand or backhand. You can also do this drill with your forehand block. However, you don't want to get in the habit of blocking too much with the forehand because it's better to go for more aggressive shots on the forehand side.

Success Goal = 20 consecutive backhand blocks, side to side

Your Score = (#) _____ consecutive backhand blocks, side to side

3. *Random Blocking*

Have your partner attack to all parts of the table. Return each shot with either your forehand or your backhand block. Here, you're learning the transition between your forehand and backhand shots. On balls hit to the middle, you'll have to decide which side to use, but generally, when close to the table, use your backhand against strong shots to the middle.

Success Goal = 15 consecutive blocks, either forehand or backhand

Your Score = (#) _____ consecutive blocks, either forehand or backhand

4. *Block Against Forehand Attack*

Play a game to 11 with these rules. Your partner serves topspin to your forehand. You block. Partner then attacks with her forehand into your forehand block. She should hit hard, even smash, while you block the ball back. Then play a game where your partner hits forehands from the backhand corner into your backhand, also starting with a topspin serve. This simulates what is probably the most common type of rally in table tennis—one player attacking with the forehand into the other player's block.

Success Goal = Win 1 game blocking against forehand attack with the forehand or backhand block

Your Score =
   (#) _____ games won using the forehand block
   (#) _____ games won using the backhand block

5. *Forehand Hit Against Block*

Redo the previous game, except you do the forehand hitting while opponent blocks.

Success Goal = Win 1 game using the forehand attack against your partner's block

Your Score = (#) _____ games won using the forehand attack

6. Quick Blocking

Quick block backhand to backhand as many times as you can. Concentrate on blocking as quick off the bounce as possible. Then do the same with the forehand. This drill teaches you to block quickly against a slow opponent.

Success Goal = 20 consecutive backhand and 20 consecutive forehand quick blocks

Your Score =
   (#) _____ consecutive backhand quick blocks
   (#) _____ consecutive forehand quick blocks

7. Middle Drill

Your partner hits either forehands or backhands (his choice) over and over to your middle. (Your partner should aim for your playing elbow.) You have to choose each time whether to block with your forehand or backhand. Block each ball back to the same spot for your partner.

Success Goal = 10 consecutive blocks from middle

Your Score = (#) _____ consecutive blocks from middle

8. Hard-Soft Drill

Hit forehands to your partner's forehand or backhand block. Alternate between hard and soft hits. Then repeat with the backhand. In this drill you learn to adjust to different ball speeds during a rally.

Success Goal = 20 consecutive alternate hard/soft forehand hits

Your Score =
   (#) _____ consecutive alternate hard/soft forehand hits
   (#) _____ consecutive alternate hard/soft backhand hits

9. *Wide Forehand Game*

Play a game with the following rules. Server serves backspin to receiver's backhand. Receiver pushes to server's backhand. Server uses two-step footwork and steps around the backhand corner, attacking push with forehand drive to receiver's backhand. Receiver quickly backhand blocks the ball to the server's wide forehand. Server then uses two-step footwork to cover wide forehand with forehand drive or smash. Play out point. Game is to 11 points.

Success Goal = Win at least half of the games

Your Score = (#) _____ games won, (#) _____ games lost

Blocking
Keys to Success Checklist

When you develop a good blocking game, you will have confidence that you can handle any attack by your opponent. This lets you concentrate on playing your own shots, rather than worry about your opponent's shots. Remember that, in general, you don't want to block too much. Block when your opponent forces you (with a strong attack), or against an opponent who can't react to a quick block. Use drive shots whenever possible.

Have your instructor or practice partner use the Keys to Success checklist (see Figure 7.1) to verify that you're doing both forehand and backhand blocks correctly. Pay particular attention to adjusting to different speeds and spins, quickness off the bounce, and contacting the ball in the center of the racket.

Step 8   Looping: Topspin Attacking

The loop is probably the most important shot in table tennis. It's a heavy topspin shot done by just grazing the ball upward and forward. There are many types of loops—forehand and backhand, against backspin and topspin, counterloops (loops versus loops)—and they come in all speeds. Not only must you learn to loop, but you must learn to return the loop, most often with a block.

The topspin of a loop does three things:

- Makes the ball jump when it hits the table
- Makes an opponent who doesn't adjust to the topspin hit high or off the end of the table
- Pulls the ball down in flight, letting you hit the ball faster but still hit the table

There are three looping speeds: slow, medium, and fast.

The slow loop is the slowest, spinniest loop. You stroke mostly up and just barely graze the ball to give the most topspin but the least speed. The slow loop is an excellent way to set up a kill shot (a ball hit with enough speed so your opponent cannot make a return) on the next shot. But some opponents may be able to attack it. Because of the grazing contact, you may miss the ball entirely in attempting the slow loop. The shot is done mostly against backspin.

The medium loop is the safest loop, with medium speed and medium spin. It's easier than a slow loop because the contact doesn't have to be as fine. To do a medium loop, you should sink the ball into the sponge a little more than with a slow loop, creating more speed but less topspin. The stroke is more forward than the slow loop. A good setup shot, it's also a good rallying shot.

The fast loop is the most powerful and most difficult loop. A put-away shot, this loop is mostly speed but still has a lot of topspin. The ball sinks more into the sponge than with other loops, and the stroke is more forward.

With fast loops (as with all other strokes), you have to stroke more up against backspin, or more forward against topspin. Also note that against backspin, a player can use the incoming spin to create more topspin. Against topspin, the very same loop will have less spin but more speed because the incoming topspin will make the ball bounce off the racket faster.

A loop is best done with an inverted sponge, preferably a relatively new sheet. You can loop with pips, especially against backspin, but you'll have less spin than is possible with an inverted sponge.

The loop is best done with the forehand, but it can also be done with the backhand. Most players do not generate as much power on the backhand side and the shot itself is more difficult. So, in this step you will first learn the forehand loop, then the backhand loop. After you know those loops, you can try counterlooping. Then you will learn crossover footwork to cover your wide forehand.

WHY IS THE LOOP IMPORTANT?

Topspin pulls the ball down and forces opponents into errors. On a normal drive, topspin is moderate, so the effect is moderate. However, with a loop, the spin is extreme and the effect becomes maximal.

With a small amount of topspin, any ball can be hit hard. However, precision is needed on a hard shot, and it is easy to make mistakes. Even if the shot hits, an opponent who reacts fast enough will probably return it.

A loop gives you far more margin for error. The extreme topspin pulls the ball down, so even if you mis-hit, the ball may still hit the table. And your opponent has to deal not only with the speed of the ball but also with the spin.

EXECUTING THE FOREHAND LOOP

Start by facing the table, your right foot slightly back (see Figure 8.1a). Rotate your hips, waist, and shoulders backward, bringing racket and arm back. Straighten your arm until it points back and down, with your wrist cocked down. Against backspin, your arm should point more down and your knees should bend even more. Drop your right shoulder against backspin. Against topspin, point your arm more backward and slightly down. Shift your weight onto your right foot (see Figure 8.1b).

Start the forward stroke by rotating your hips and waist forward. Rotate your shoulders, pulling with the left. Just before contact, snap your forearm into the ball smoothly but vigorously. Against backspin, snap your wrist at contact. (Advanced players sometimes use wrist against topspin as well, but it's harder to control.)

Contact the ball as it drops for maximum spin and control, at the top of the bounce for faster, more aggressive loops. Contact is made in front and to the right of your body, immediately after shoulder and hip rotation. Whip the racket around the outside of the ball, closing it as you do so to create spin (see Figure 8.1c). Contact is a grazing motion. Contact should be made on the top half of the racket, toward the tip. Against backspin, contact the back of the ball. Against topspin, contact the back top of the ball.

Arm should continue up and forward, finishing with the racket somewhere around the forehead or higher (see Figure 8.1d). Transfer your weight to your left foot. Return to ready position.

Figure 8.1   Keys to Success: Forehand Loop

Preparation Phase

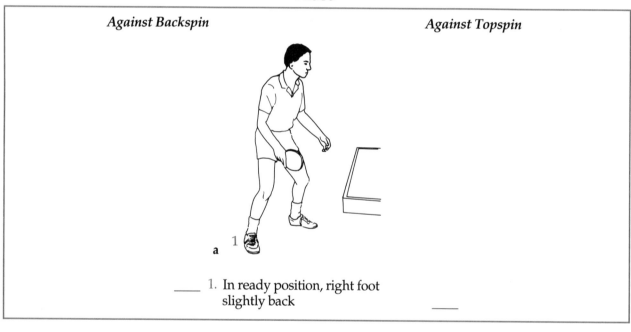

Against Backspin

Against Topspin

_____ 1. In ready position, right foot slightly back

_____

Execution
Phase

Backswing

Against Backspin   *Against Topspin*

_____ 1. Rotate body back and down on waist, hips, and shoulders   _____

2. Both knees well bent, with back knee bent more than front knee _____
3. Racket tip and arm point mostly down _____

2. Both knees only slightly bent _____
3. Racket tip and arm point backward and slightly down _____

_____ 4. Weight shifts to back foot   _____
_____ 5. Wrist cocked slightly down   _____

Forward Swing

Against Backspin   *Against Topspin*

1. Push up and forward with legs _____

1. Push forward with legs _____

_____ 2. Rotate hips, waist, and shoulders forward
_____ 3. Snap arm at elbow   _____
_____ 4. Weight transfers to front foot   _____

Against Backspin	*Against Topspin*
5. Snap wrist at contact ____	5. Optional wrist snap ____
6. Power should be aimed mostly upward, especially for extra topspin; more forward for speed ____	6. Power should be aimed mostly forward ____
7. Contact ball on the drop ____	7. Contact ball on drop or top of bounce ____
8. Graze ball at contact ____	8. Graze ball at contact somewhat, but ball sinks into sponge ____

____ 9. Accelerate throughout shot   ____

Follow-Through Phase

Against Backspin	*Against Topspin*

____ 1. Follow through naturally, upward and forward, with racket continuing the motion ____
____ 2. Return to ready position ____

EXECUTING THE BACKHAND LOOP

Start by facing the table (see Figure 8.2a) with your legs slightly wider than normal. Against backspin, backswing almost straight down between your legs, tip down, and bend your knees. Against topspin, backswing to your left hip.

Drop your right shoulder slightly. Rotate your hips to the left, shifting some weight to your left foot. Lean your upper body forward slightly. Cock your wrist back (see Figure 8.2b).

Let the ball drop some, especially against backspin. Against backspin, begin your forward swing by lifting your upper body; this lifts your arm. Against topspin, begin your forward swing by rotating your hips forward.

Pull the racket forward using first your shoulder, then your elbow (see Figure 8.2c). Snap your wrist into the ball at contact. Rotate the racket around the ball, closing the racket as you do so to create topspin. The more you graze the ball, the more spin and the less speed you get, and vice versa. Make contact on the top half of the racket. Shift your weight to the right foot. Against backspin, contact the back of the ball. Against topspin, contact the back top of the ball.

Follow through naturally, letting the racket go forward and up (see Figure 8.2d). Racket should point a little to the right of where the ball is going. Return to ready position.

Figure 8.2 Keys to Success: *Backhand Loop*

Preparation Phase

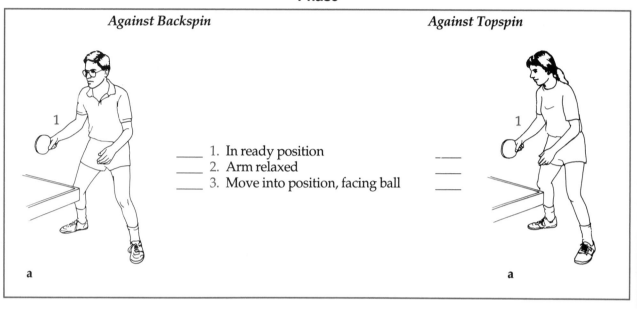

Against Backspin   *Against Topspin*

_____ 1. In ready position
_____ 2. Arm relaxed
_____ 3. Move into position, facing ball

a   a

Execution Phase

Backswing

Against Backspin   *Against Topspin*

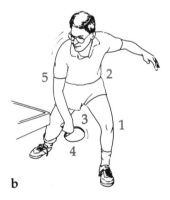   

b   b

1. Bend knees _____
2. Rotate hips slightly to left _____
3. Drop arm between legs _____
4. Racket tip points down _____
5. Drop right shoulder slightly forward and down _____

1. Rotate hips slightly to left _____
2. Racket backswings to left thigh _____
3. Racket points down and back _____
4. Drop right shoulder slightly forward and down _____

Forward Swing

Against Backspin

Against Topspin

c

c

1. Push up with legs and waist ____
2. Drive racket upward and forward with arm and shoulder ____
3. Contact ball on drop ____
4. Graze ball ____
5. Power should go mostly upward ____

1. Rotate hips forward ____
2. Drive racket forward with arm and shoulder ____
3. Contact ball on the drop or top of bounce ____
4. Graze ball at contact somewhat, but ball sinks into sponge ____
5. Power should go mostly forward ____

____ 6. Snap wrist just before contact ____
____ 7. Accelerate throughout stroke ____

Follow-Through Phase

Against Backspin

Against Topspin

d

____ 1. Follow through naturally, upward and forward
____ 2. Return to ready position

____
____

d

COUNTERLOOPING

The counterloop is a loop against a loop. It's more difficult (and therefore more fun!) to learn, and it's widely used at the highest levels. It can be done either forehand or backhand, but it's more difficult and challenging to do backhand. To counterloop, just use a normal loop against top-spin as described earlier, only you'll be doing it farther away from the table than normal, against a much heavier topspin. If you do contact the ball farther away from the table than normal, topspin and gravity will have more time to pull the ball down, increasing your consistency but giving your opponent more time to react.

At first, take the ball well after the top of the bounce. Go for as much spin as possible. As you get better, try taking the ball a little closer to the table. The closer you are to the table when you counterloop, the more trouble your opponent will have in return-ing it. Some players have even perfected looping right off the bounce.

Detecting Loop Errors

Looping is one of the most complex of table tennis strokes. Therefore, it's especially important that you examine the way you're doing the shot. More than with any other shot, if you do one part of the loop wrong, you'll do the rest of it wrong. When done correctly, the loop is one of the most natural of shots.

ERROR

CORRECTION

1. The ball goes into the net or off the end.

2. You're off balance.

3. You're not getting enough spin.

4. You're missing the ball completely.

5. You're hitting the racket edge.

6. You're having trouble overcoming the backspin and lifting the ball over the net.

1. Read the spin and adjust the racket angle. Stroke up more against backspin.

2. Move to the ball, don't reach.

3. Make sure you're grazing the ball. Accelerate into the ball, using all parts of the stroke. Relax your arm for more acceleration.

4. Due to the grazing motion, this will happen sometimes. Make sure the grazing motion isn't too precise. Keep your eye on the ball.

5. Approach the ball with a slightly more open racket; close it at contact.

6. Bend your knees, get down low, and aim your power upward with a more open racket. Relax your muscles.

CROSSOVERS

Since a looper is often several steps away from the table (unlike a hitter, who usually stays close), a looper has more ground to cover. Often a looper will forehand loop from the backhand corner, and if the opponent blocks this to the wide forehand, the looper has a long way to go. A looper could use regular two-step footwork, but a more efficient method in this case is crossover footwork.

Crossover footwork is good for covering a lot of ground, especially toward the forehand side. It puts you in perfect position to use full power on the forehand shot, whether it be a loop or drive. Crossover footwork may leave you in poor position to hit the next shot compared to two-step footwork, so returning to ready position quickly is important. (However, this is offset by the fact that crossover footwork enables you to put so much power into the shot that the ball usually doesn't come back.) Crossover footwork is used successfully by most top players, especially loopers with strong forehands. Hitters also use crossover footwork sometimes, but since they usually don't have as much ground to cover, they use it less often, and many

don't use it at all. Nearly all high level players who loop use crossover footwork.

HOW TO EXECUTE CROSSOVER FOOTWORK

Crossover footwork is used mostly after hitting a forehand from the backhand corner. You are now way out of position and vulnerable to a quick shot to the wide forehand. You could use two-step footwork, but that might not cover enough ground.

Instead you may elect to use a crossover. To do so, start with a short step with the right foot as with two-step footwork (see Figure 8.3). Then simply cross your left foot over your right, pivoting your body so your legs don't actually cross. Try it and you'll see.

Your body should be rotated so that it points sideways or even a little backward. Uncoil your body as you rotate into the shot, and you'll get surprising power. After taking your shot, get back into position as fast as possible because you're now vulnerable on the backhand side.

Figure 8.3 Keys to Success: *Crossover Footwork*

(Moving to the right—reverse right and left to move to the left)

Preparation Phase

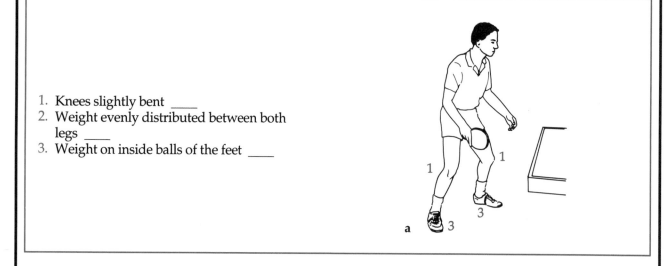

1. Knees slightly bent ____
2. Weight evenly distributed between both legs ____
3. Weight on inside balls of the feet ____

Execution Phase

1. Right foot short steps ____
2. Weight shifts to right foot ____
3. Entire body pivots to right as left leg crosses over ____

b   2

c   3

Follow-Through Phase

1. End in position for stroke ____
2. Start stroke immediately ____

d

BLOCKING THE LOOP

Earlier, you learned how to block. However, when you first try blocking the loop, you'll undoubtedly block the ball off the end. This is because of the heavy topspin. You'll have to close your racket.

Aim for the bottom of the net or even lower (see Figure 8.4). The ball should sink deep into the sponge, all the way to the wood. The incoming topspin will make the ball jump off the racket, so not much forward motion is needed.

Make sure to take the ball quick off the bounce. Otherwise, the ball will jump too fast for you to react to it. By taking it quickly, the ball can't jump too far too fast. Also, a quick return doesn't give your opponent much time to react.

When blocking the loop, remember to

- close the racket,
- take the ball quickly, while it's rising, and
- use the incoming topspin to produce speed.

Figure 8.4   Aim low when blocking the loop.

Looping Drills

1. Loop Against Bounced Ball

Standing on your side of the table, drop a ball on the floor so that it bounces about waist-high. Loop the ball on the table. This is an easy way to practice the loop stroke against a predictable ball.

Success Goal = 15 consecutive forehand loops, 15 consecutive backhand loops

Your Score =

(#) _____ consecutive forehand loops against bounced ball

(#) _____ consecutive backhand loops against bounced ball

2. Loop Against Backspin

Serve backspin to your partner. Have him push it back to your forehand. Loop the ball with your forehand. Your partner blocks the ball back; you catch it and start over. Then do the same with the backhand loop, with your partner pushing to your backhand side. Then do the same, this time looping your forehand out of your backhand corner against your partner's push. This is not only a good way to practice your loop against backspin, it's the most common way rallies start in a game—one player serves backspin, the other pushes it back, and the server loops. (The most common thing a coach tells a player is to serve backspin and loop, because most players are unable to push short consistently and are unwilling to flip the ball—an aggressive return of a short ball and a higher-risk shot—see Step 9).

Success Goal = 15 forehand loops from forehand side, 15 backhand loops from backhand side, and 15 forehand loops from backhand side

Your Score =

(#) _____ forehand loops against backspin from forehand side

(#) _____ backhand loops against backspin from backhand side

(#) _____ forehand loops against backspin from backhand side

3. *Loop Against Block*

Serve topspin to your partner's forehand, or have your partner serve topspin to your forehand. Your partner blocks while you loop forehands crosscourt. Then do the same thing with the backhand loop, this time going crosscourt backhand to backhand. (You can also do this drill down the line.) This drill will help you develop a consistent loop stroke that can be used in a match situation.

Success Goal = 15 consecutive forehand and 15 consecutive backhand loops against block

Your Score =

(#) _____ consecutive forehand loops against block

(#) _____ consecutive backhand loops against block

4. *Blocking the Loop*

Have your partner loop over and over to your backhand with either a forehand or backhand loop. (Forehand loop can be done from either the backhand corner or forehand corner into your backhand.) Then have your partner loop forehands from his or her forehand corner to your forehand. You should return the ball by using a block. This drill will help you develop a consistent block against heavy topspin.

Success Goal = 15 consecutive backhand and 15 consecutive forehand blocks

Your Score =

(#) _____ consecutive backhand blocks

(#) _____ consecutive forehand blocks

5. *Loop Against Backspin/Topspin*

Serve backspin. Your partner pushes to your forehand. Loop your forehand crosscourt. Your partner blocks crosscourt; rally continues, with you looping and your partner blocking. You can also try this with the backhand loop, but that's more difficult. This drill teaches you to adjust your racket angle when looping against different spins and shots.

Success Goal = 15 consecutive forehand loops, starting against backspin and continuing against block

Your Score = (#) _____ consecutive forehand loops

6. *Crossover Footwork*

Your partner hits to your wide forehand. Starting in your backhand corner, do a crossover. Walk back to your backhand corner and repeat. This will help you become familiar with the crossover.

Success Goal = Move to wide forehand 10 times correctly, using crossover footwork

Your Score = (#) _____ correct repetitions

7. *Crossovers Against Block*

Stand in your backhand corner and serve topspin to your partner's forehand. Your partner drives medium hard to your wide forehand. Use a crossover to get to the ball. While you're learning the crossover, use a drive. When you're comfortable with the footwork, combine it with looping, and loop your partner's drive. Play out the rally. This simulates the situation you will often face after attacking with your forehand out of your backhand corner.

Success Goal = 10 returns in a row with a crossover

Your Score = (#) _____ returns made consecutively after crossover

8. *Crossover and Loop*

Play a game with the following rules. The rally starts with the server serving backspin to receiver's backhand. Receiver pushes it to server's backhand corner. Server steps around with two-step footwork and loops forehand to backhand corner. Receiver blocks the ball to server's wide forehand. Server uses a crossover to get to the ball and loops it. Play out the point. Games are to 11 points.

Success Goal = Win at least half the games played

Your Score = (#) _____ wins, (#) _____ losses

9. *Random Backspin Serve and Loop*

Play a game with the following rules. You serve backspin. Your partner pushes it back anywhere. You loop either backhand or forehand, depending on where the push goes. Play out the point. More rallies start with this sequence than any other way. One of the quickest ways to improve at table tennis is to perfect a serve-and-loop game, with most of your serves being short backspin combined with sidespin.

Success Goal = Win at least half the games played

Your Score = (#) _____ wins, (#) _____ losses

10. *Alternate Forehand and Backhand Loops*

Partner blocks side to side (left and right) while you loop. Some players may wish to loop the forehand and drive the backhand.

Success Goal = 15 consecutive repetitions of forehand and backhand alternate loops (or backhand hits)

Your Score = (#) _____ consecutive repetitions of forehand and backhand alternate loops (or backhand hits)

11. *Loop and Smash*

Serve backspin. Your partner pushes to your backhand corner. You loop either forehand or backhand to your partner's backhand. Your partner blocks the ball back to your backhand. You smash, either forehand or backhand. See how many you can make in a row.

Success Goal = 10 consecutive loop/smash combinations

Your Score = (#) _____ consecutive loop/smash combinations

12. *Forehand Counterloop*

Both players loop forehands back and forth. (This is a more advanced drill.) Try for consistency by backing off the table and taking the ball as it drops. If you go off the end, remember not to lift—the ball has heavy topspin. (This is a common type of rally among advanced players.)

Success Goal = 5 consecutive forehand counterloops

Your Score = (#) _____ consecutive forehand counterloops

Looping
Keys to Success Checklists

The biggest difference between looping against backspin versus looping against topspin is the direction of force. Against backspin, your force goes mostly upward and a little forward. But against topspin, or block, it goes mostly forward and slightly upward. Don't fall into the habit of learning one but not the other.

Remember to keep your arm loose and make a complete stroke. When learning a new stroke, many players tense up, and this will especially hurt your loop stroke. Players who have trouble looping at first often shorten their new stroke. This is a big mistake because it severely limits the amount of topspin you can produce.

Have your instructor or practice partner use the Keys to Success checklists (see Figures 8.1 and 8.2) to verify that you are doing both the forehand and backhand loops correctly. Pay particular attention to the differences between looping against backspin (as opposed to topspin), to contact, and to the sequence of motions in the strokes, all of which have to be done smoothly and in the proper order. Use the Crossover Keys to Success checklist (see Figure 8.3) to make sure you're moving to the wide forehand properly.

Step 9   # Flipping: How to Attack Short Balls

The flip is an aggressive return of a short ball—a ball that would land on your side of the table twice if given the chance. It's most often used against short serves and short pushes. On the backhand side, the flip is basically the same as a backhand drive, but on the forehand it's different.

A flip can be done either crosscourt, down the line, or to the middle. Flip to your opponent's weaker side most of the time (usually down the line to the backhand), but usually go crosscourt whenever you go for a very aggressive flip (so you'll have more margin for error). An aggressive flip to a player's middle (elbow) is also very effective, because your opponent may have trouble deciding whether to return with a forehand or a backhand.

A flip is done against a ball that has landed short. If it lands short on the forehand side, it can be awkward to reach. For this shot, you'll also need to learn stepping-in footwork.

WHY IS THE FLIP IMPORTANT?

You could use a normal forehand drive against a short ball to the forehand, but it would be awkward because the table is in the way. A flip is less awkward and more deceptive. But don't overuse the flip; just the threat of it makes your other returns more effective. Too many flips and your opponent gets used to them.

EXECUTING THE FLIP

When your opponent serves or pushes short, you'll have to step in to flip. If you reach over the table you'll be off balance and have trouble controlling the shot, especially if you're short. Even tall players have to step in, or they too will not hit their best shot. Most players have little trouble reaching a ball short to their backhand but find it very awkward to deal with the short one to the forehand unless they step in.

If you're a step or so away from the table, step forward first with your left leg, getting it close to the endline. If you're already close, don't move the left leg. The longer your legs are, the easier stepping in will be.

Step in with your right leg under the table and toward the ball. Get the leg as far under the table as you can comfortably. Most of your weight should now be on the right foot (see Figure 9.1a). Reach over the table with the racket, with your body facing where the contact will be. Against backspin, cock your wrist down and open the racket; otherwise, cock your wrist straight back and keep the racket perpendicular to the floor. Bring the racket to a position just behind the contact point (see Figure 9.1b).

Bring the racket forward with your elbow. Then snap your wrist forward (and slightly up against backspin). Your wrist should rotate at contact, which closes the racket some. Contact should be an upward grazing motion against backspin for control, or straight through and forward against topspin or for extra speed (see Figure 9.1, c and d). The stroke against backspin and topspin is essentially the same, but you should open your racket more and stroke slightly up against backspin.

Contact should be on the back bottom of the ball against backspin, on the back or top back of the ball against other spins. Make sure to contact the ball directly opposite where you want it to go. When flipping, make sure to flip to wide angles—either crosscourt at a wide angle or straight down the line (unless you go after your opponent's middle). Step back quickly, and return to ready position.

If the ball you're flipping is high, "flip kill" it. This is just a flip at full power. Use both wrist and elbow snap for power, and go crosscourt so you'll have more room.

Figure 9.1　Keys to Success: Forehand Flipping

Preparation Phase

1. Step right foot under table ____
2. Weight goes to right foot ____
3. Upper body faces ball ____

a

Execution Phase

Backswing

1. Bring racket just behind ball ____
2. Against backspin, open racket ____
3. Against topspin, racket should be straight ____
4. Tilt wrist backward ____

b

Forward Swing

1. Snap wrist and elbow ____
2. Against backspin, stroke slightly upward with grazing motion, rotating racket around ball ____
3. Against topspin or for more speed, contact straight on ____
4. Contact at top of bounce or earlier ____
5. Ball should go to very wide forehand or down line, or at opponent's middle ____

c

Follow-Through Phase

1. Follow through naturally, forward ____
2. Step back quickly into ready position ____

d

Detecting Flipping Errors

Flipping is a simple motion, with only a few possible errors. Make sure you step in properly, get your racket into position, and make the right type of contact. The rest is all timing.

ERROR

CORRECTION

1. The ball goes into the net when flipping against backspin.

2. The ball goes off the end when flipping against topspin.

3. You have difficulty flipping down the line.

4. You're off balance.

1. Open your racket and stroke upward, topspinning the ball. Get racket under the ball, especially against heavy backspin.

2. Close your racket and make sure you aren't stroking upward—stroke straight forward.

3. Make sure your upper body faces the ball. Bring the wrist backward and contact the back of the ball, not the right side.

4. Make sure to step in.

Flipping Drills

1. Stepping-In Footwork

Put your racket on the table on your forehand side near the net. Then, using stepping-in footwork, reach in and pick it up. Step back quickly; repeat, this time putting the racket back. Make sure to stay balanced. This simulates the movement you'll make when you reach in to flip a short ball to the forehand.

Success Goal = Step in and out quickly 20 times correctly

Your Score = (#) _____ correct repetitions

2. Forehand Flip

Have your partner serve short no-spin serves to your forehand. Flip the ball crosscourt, then down the line. Your partner catches the ball and serves again. Hit the right side of the ball to flip to the left (crosscourt), and hit the back of the ball to go to the right (down the line). This teaches you the proper racket angles for going down both lines, without having to adjust for spin.

Success Goal = 15 consecutive flips down each line

Your Score =
   (#) _____ consecutive flips crosscourt
   (#) _____ consecutive flips down the line

3. Flipping Topspin and Backspin

Have your partner serve first topspin and then backspin serves short to your forehand. Flip the ball. Your partner catches the ball and serves again. Now you're beginning to learn to adjust to different spins by adjusting your racket angle and stroke.

Success Goal = Against topspin, 15 consecutive flips both crosscourt and down the line; against backspin, the same

Your Score =
   a. Against topspin
      (#) _____ consecutive flips crosscourt
      (#) _____ consecutive flips down the line
   b. Against backspin
      (#) _____ consecutive flips crosscourt
      (#) _____ consecutive flips down the line

4. *Alternate Flip and Short Push*

Your partner serves short backspin to your forehand. You alternate flipping and short push. Your partner catches the ball and serves again. This gives you a double threat: Your opponent has to be ready for a flip that goes deep or a push that goes short—and it's tricky guarding against both these shots.

Success Goal = 20 successful consecutive returns, alternating between short push and flip

Your Score = (#) _____ successful consecutive returns, alternating between short push and flip

5. *Attack After Flip*

Your partner serves short to your forehand. You flip crosscourt and get back into position quickly. Your partner counterdrives or blocks back to your forehand. You attack crosscourt against your partner's forehand block for the rest of the rally. This is good practice for following up your flip with an attack. Because a flip brings you over the table, it isn't always easy to recover for the next shot.

Success Goal = 10 consecutive attacking shots, starting against a flip

Your Score = (#) _____ consecutive loops, starting against a flip

6. *Flip and Attack*

Play games to 11 points where your partner always serves short to your forehand, mixing up the spin. Flip anywhere, and play out the point. This is similar to what you will face in a real match.

Success Goal = Win at least half of the games played

Your Score = (#) _____ games won, (#) _____ games lost

7. *Flip Against Short Push Game*

Play games to 11 points where you serve short backspin anywhere. Your partner pushes short anywhere. You attack with either a forehand flip or a backhand drive, depending on where your partner's push is. Play out the point. In a match situation, the player who attacks first (and most effectively) usually wins.

Success Goal = Win at least half of the games played

Your Score = (#) _____ games won, (#) _____ games lost

8. *Flip or Loop Game*

Play games to 11 points with the following rules. You serve short backspin. Your partner pushes either short to forehand or long anywhere. You either flip forehand or loop (or drive) either backhand or forehand. Play out the point.

Success Goal = Win at least half of the games played

Your Score = (#) _____ games won, (#) _____ games lost

9. *Flip Kill*

You serve short backspin. Your partner pushes short to your forehand, slightly high. You flip kill crosscourt. This drill teaches you how to kill a ball that is high, but short on your forehand side. If you learn this well, your opponent will think twice about going short to your forehand.

Success Goal = 10 consecutive flip kills

Your Score = (#) _____ consecutive flip kills

Flipping
Keys to Success Checklist

Stepping in is one of the more overlooked aspects of executing the flip. Remember to step well under the table so that you are balanced as you make the shot. The shot itself should be short and placed down both lines, quick off the bounce. Placement is important, so make sure you can flip the ball to either wide corner. You don't want your opponent to have time to react!

To help you perfect your flip, have your instructor or practice partner verify with the Keys to Success checklist (see Figure 9.1) that you're doing the forehand flip correctly. Have them pay particular attention to the way you step in and to your balance during the shot. Also have them critique your placement—make sure your shots go to wide angles, not to the middle of the table, unless done intentionally.

Step 10   Chopping: Backspin Defense

Chopping is a defensive return of a drive with backspin. Most choppers back up 5 to 15 feet from the table, returning the ball low with variable backspin. There aren't as many good choppers nowadays as there used to be, mostly due to the loop drive; however, the style still persists. A number of players have developed games that combine chopping with another style (such as looping). This step will help you learn both how to chop and how to chop the loop.

There are three ways a player can win points when chopping (aside from a lucky edge or net!):

- *Outlasting an opponent.* Simply chop every drive back until the opponent makes an error.
- *Forcing an error.* Mix up spins or put so much backspin on the ball that the opponent makes a mistake.
- *Attacking.* Look for a weak drive or drop shot and attack, catching the opponent off guard.

Generally, the chop strokes are used either by an all-around player as a variation, or by a chop specialist who uses it over and over (at least until that player finds a chance to attack!).

A chopper should be aware of the expedite rule, since it may affect his or her style. Before the expedite rule, there were often matches between two choppers that would last for hours. (One point at the World Championships lasted almost three hours.) Under modern rules, if any individual game is not complete after 15 minutes (not including official breaks), the expedite rule comes into play for the rest of the match. Under the expedite rule, players alternate serves, and the server has to win the point within 13 shots (including the serve). If the receiver makes 13 consecutive returns in the rally, the receiver wins the point. If a chopper is in a match that is approaching the expedite rule time limit, he or she should attack more and try to end the game before the expedite rule takes over.

WHY IS CHOPPING IMPORTANT?

Chopping is one of the few strokes that you don't absolutely need, although it will help as a variation even if you use it only occasionally. However, many defensive players specialize in chopping. The idea behind chopping is that if you can chop all of your opponent's drives back, he or she can't score. If you can further force errors by extreme backspin, by spin variations, by mixing in attacks, or by simply getting everything back until your opponent misses, you can score. If you're an attacker, you'll sometimes find yourself out of position, and a good chop will often get you back into the point.

EXECUTING THE CHOP

Since the forehand and backhand chops obey the same fundamentals, they'll be introduced together.

Start in a chopper's ready position, with your right foot slightly in front (see Figure 10.1a). Bend your knees, especially on the backhand chop. Rotate your body to the left for the backhand chop, to the right for the forehand chop. For the forehand chop, bring your right foot back slightly. For the backhand chop, bring your left foot back slightly. Make sure to backswing early—early racket preparation is important.

Transfer some weight to the back foot. Bring your arm back and slightly up. Racket should be open, and your wrist cocked back (see Figure 10.1b).

Using your elbow, bring the racket down and forward to the ball. Graze the bottom back of the ball. Contact should be made after the ball has dropped to about table level, lower against heavy topspin (see Figure 10.1c). Use a light touch—this is a defensive shot, not a fast one. The ball should travel slowly.

Follow through forward and slightly downward until your arm is almost straight (see Figure 10.1d). There should be some weight shift to the front foot. Return to ready position.

Figure 10.1   *Keys to Success:*
Forehand and Backhand Chops

**Preparation
Phase**

Forehand Chop   *Backhand Chop*

a

____   1. In ready position, right foot slightly
            in front
____   2. Arm relaxed   ____
____   3. Move into position   ____

**Execution
Phase**

Backswing

Forehand Chop   *Backhand Chop*

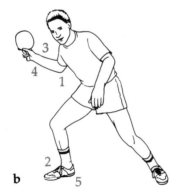   

b   b

1. Rotate hips and waist to the   1. Rotate hips and waist to the
   right ____   left ____
2. Bring right foot back ____   2. Bring left foot back ____

          ____   3. Bring arm up and back   ____
          ____   4. Cock wrist back   ____
          ____   5. Most weight shifts to back foot ____

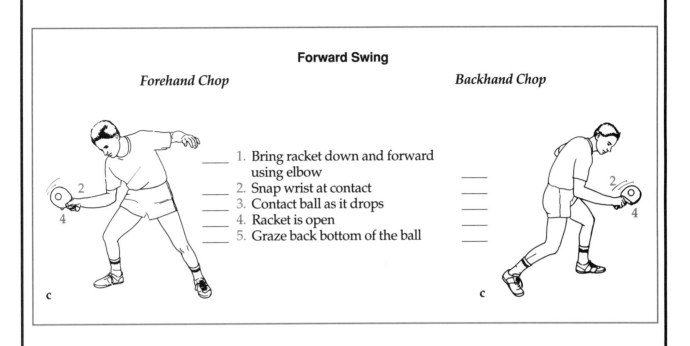

Forward Swing

Forehand Chop   *Backhand Chop*

_____ 1. Bring racket down and forward
         using elbow   _____
_____ 2. Snap wrist at contact   _____
_____ 3. Contact ball as it drops   _____
_____ 4. Racket is open   _____
_____ 5. Graze back bottom of the ball   _____

**Follow-Through
Phase**

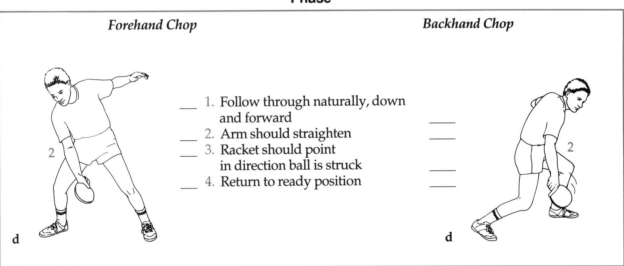

Forehand Chop   *Backhand Chop*

___ 1. Follow through naturally, down
       and forward
___ 2. Arm should straighten   _____
___ 3. Racket should point   _____
       in direction ball is struck
___ 4. Return to ready position   _____

CHOPPING THE LOOP

Against a loop, you have to adjust for the extra topspin or your return will pop up or go off the end. Take the ball a little lower and have your racket a little less closed. You will need to contact the ball lower, so bend down low and bend your knees (see Figure 10.2). You may want to chop down more vigorously to overcome the spin, but do so smoothly. Contact should be more behind and less under the ball.

Figure 10.2   Bend down low to chop the loop.

Detecting Forehand and Backhand Chopping Errors

A chopper can be thought of as a machine. If well-oiled, a machine is flawless, and similarly, a chopper's defense must be flawless. It only takes a minor mistake for the machine to fail, and similarly, a chopper has to do everything correctly, or the shot falls apart. With most other shots, a player can do something incorrectly and still get away with it for a time (which leads to players not making necessary changes until the bad habits are ingrained). Choppers, however, have to be precise, or they can't even keep the ball in play. Fortunately, most chopping errors are fairly obvious and easy to correct.

ERROR

CORRECTION

ERROR	CORRECTION
1. The ball pops up.	1. Close the racket, or let the ball drop more before contact. There may be more topspin on it than you think. Against heavy topspin, let the ball drop more and contact it more behind, less underneath.
2. The ball goes into the net	2. Open the racket. There may not be as much topspin on the ball as you think.
3. You can't react to the shot.	3. You may be too close to the table. Back up and give yourself more time. Choppers typically return shots from 5 to 15 feet back.
4. You're not using enough backspin.	4. Make sure you're grazing the ball. One option is to snap your wrist to increase spin, but reduce control. As you improve, snap your wrist more for extra spin.
5. Your backhand chop stroke is too short and jerky.	5. Turn more sideways to allow room for your backswing, and take a longer backswing.
6. You're off balance.	6. Move to the ball, don't reach.

Chopping Drills

1. Chopping Against a Wall

Find a wall with a hard floor next to it. Drop a ball on the floor and chop it against the wall after it bounces. When the ball bounces back, chop it against the wall again. You might also draw a line on the wall 3 feet from the ground, the height of the net. Try to chop the ball a few inches above the line each time. This is an easy way to develop your chop without the uncertainties of an actual rally. Ten-time U.S. National Men's Champion Richard Miles, the best chopper in U.S. history (and one of the very best ever) developed his chop this way.

Success Goal = 30 consecutive forehand and 30 consecutive backhand chops

Your Score =

(#) _____ consecutive forehand chops

(#) _____ consecutive backhand chops

2. Chopping Topspin Serve

Have your partner serve topspin to your forehand. Chop it back. Your partner catches it and starts over. Then do the same with your backhand. This enables you to practice the shot without having to worry about the following shot. Make sure each shot is correct and precise—be a perfectionist.

Success Goal = 30 consecutive forehand and 30 consecutive backhand chops

Your Score =

(#) _____ consecutive forehand chops

(#) _____ consecutive backhand chops

3. Chopping a Drive

Have your partner drive with his forehand to your forehand. Chop the ball back. Then have your partner attack with his forehand to your backhand chop. (You can also have your partner attack with a backhand, but in actual match play, 90 percent of attacks against backspin—especially against choppers—are done with the forehand.)

Success Goal = 15 consecutive forehand and 15 consecutive backhand chops

Your Score =

(#) _____ consecutive forehand chops

(#) _____ consecutive backhand chops

4. Forehand/Backhand Alternate Chopping

Have your opponent drive with her forehand to your forehand side, then your backhand side. You alternate chopping forehands and backhands, using chopper's footwork. This lets you simulate the actual movements you would use against an opponent who attacks to both sides in a game.

Success Goal = 15 consecutive chops

Your Score = (#) _____ consecutive chops, alternating

5. Random Chopping

Have your opponent drive with her forehand to all parts of the table randomly. Chop with either your forehand or backhand. This is exactly what a chopper will face in a match against a strong attacker.

Success Goal = 15 consecutive chops

Your Score = (#) _____ consecutive chops

6. Chopping the Loop

Have your partner loop to your forehand. You chop and rally continues, all crosscourt. Then do the same with your backhand chop, with your partner attacking using his forehand into your backhand, crosscourt from his backhand side.

Success Goal = 10 consecutive chops against the loop, forehand and backhand

Your Score =

(#) _____ consecutive forehand chops

(#) _____ consecutive backhand chops

7. *Chopping Game*

Play games to 11 points where your partner serves topspin to your forehand. You chop crosscourt, and your partner attacks with forehand crosscourt, either hitting or looping. (No pushing allowed!) Rally continues this way, all crosscourt, until someone misses or hits to the wrong side.

Success Goal = Win at least half of the games

Your Score = (#) _____ games won, (#) _____ games lost

8. *Chop and Push Game*

Play games to 11 points where your partner alternates attacking and dropshotting to your forehand, which is how many players play choppers. You move in and out, chopping and pushing. If the drop shot goes high, smash. If you do attack in this game, you have to hit a winning shot on the first try, or your partner wins the point! This forces you to win on your chopping alone (which choppers must have confidence in to be successful), and it also reinforces the idea that when a chopper attacks, the game is won by surprise because the point must be won quickly, before the opponent recovers.

Success Goal = Win at least half of the games

Your Score = (#) _____ games won, (#) _____ games lost

Chopping
Keys to Success Checklist

The most important thing for a chopper to learn is confidence. Develop precise chopping strokes and footwork, and then your confidence will grow. Choppers who really believe they can chop back more balls than opponents can attack have already very nearly won.

Have your instructor or practice partner verify that you're doing both the forehand and back-hand strokes properly, according to the Keys to Success checklist (see Figure 10.1). Have them be perfectionists—get the stroke down perfectly. Pay particular attention to bending at the knees, especially for the backhand, and adjusting for different spins.

Step 11   Lobbing: How to Return Smashes

Lobbing is a totally defensive shot done against a smash. A good lob (which, done by the best players, is basically a high loop) can go 15 feet or more in the air, has lots of topspin or sidespin, and lands deep on the table. (Some players lob lower but with more spin.) The ball then bounces outward and high, and it might not come down until it's 10 feet past the table! This makes it difficult to smash, since the far side of the table is so far away and the ball has so much spin. If it's smashed, the lobber has a lot of time to react because the shot is coming from so far away. However, good players rarely miss smashes, and even the best lobbers almost always lose more points than they win lobbing. It is recommended that lobbing be kept to a minimum, at least if you want to win! But lobbing is fun, so don't restrict it too much.

Lobbing is similar to chopping as far as winning points. There are three ways to win a point when lobbing:

- *Outlasting an opponent.* Simply lob every drive back until the opponent makes an error.
- *Forcing an error.* Mix up spins or put so much spin on the ball that the opponent makes a mistake.
- *Attacking.* Look for every chance to counter-attack.

Many players lose points lobbing because they lob balls they shouldn't. In this step you will learn how to lob as well as how to smash or smother kill against a lob. Remember, only lob when forced to—when your opponent is smashing!

WHY IS LOBBING IMPORTANT?

Between players of roughly equal levels, most games are decided by three or fewer points. Therefore, scoring even one extra point in a game means you're a third of the way toward winning it! So even if you only score one or two points each game by lobbing, it's worth it. After all, what have you got to lose? You only lob when the opponent makes a strong smash, so if you don't lob, you're going to lose the point anyway. Besides, lobbing is the most fun part of the game!

EXECUTING THE LOB

On the forehand lob, your right foot should go back slightly, and your upper body should rotate to the right; on the backhand, do the reverse. On all lobs, bend your knees and drop the racket low (see Figure 11.1, a-d).

Open the racket slightly and get it underneath the incoming ball. Stroke mostly upward, using the same stroke you learned when looping forehands and backhands (Step 8). A lob is essentially a high loop.

If you're in trouble, you may not be able to do the stroke as explained in the looping section. After all, the incoming ball is a smash! Even though you might be rushed, try to do the entire stroke; improvise when necessary. Make sure to hit the ball high in the air with topspin. By grazing the far side of the ball (especially on the forehand side), you can also produce a sidespin that will give many players trouble.

Figure 11.1   **Keys to Success:**
Forehand and Backhand Lobs

**Preparation
Phase**

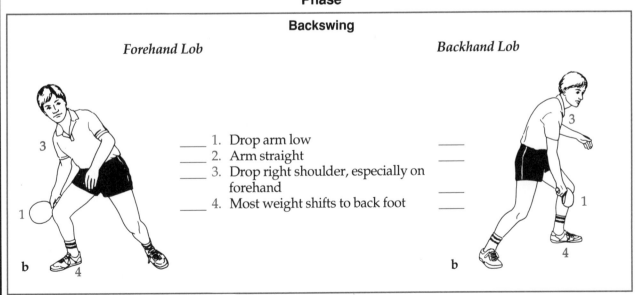

Forehand Lob   Backhand Lob

_____ 1. In ready position, about 15 to
           25 feet from table   _____
_____ 2. Arm relaxed   _____
       3. Move into position as opponent
           hits ball:

a. Rotate hips and waist to the   a. Rotate hips and waist to the
   right _____   left _____
b. Bring right foot back _____   b. Bring left foot back _____

**Execution
Phase**

Backswing

Forehand Lob   Backhand Lob

_____ 1. Drop arm low   _____
_____ 2. Arm straight   _____
_____ 3. Drop right shoulder, especially on
           forehand   _____
_____ 4. Most weight shifts to back foot   _____

Forward Swing

Forehand Lob   *Backhand Lob*

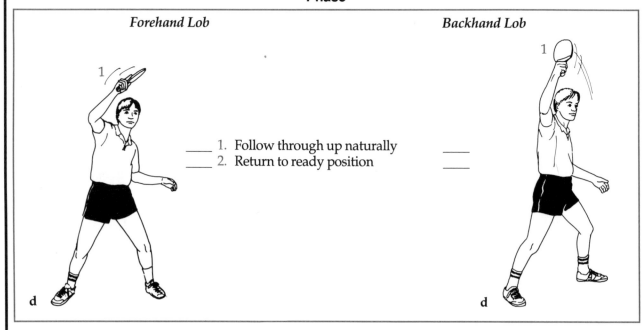

c   c

_____ 1. Push off with legs   _____
_____ 2. Stroke with elbow and shoulder   _____
_____ 3. Stroke mostly upward   _____
_____ 4. Graze back bottom of ball at
            contact   _____
_____ 5. Contact ball on drop, well away
            from table   _____
_____ 6. Hit ball high into air with topspin   _____
_____ 7. Lob should land deep on table   _____

Follow-Through
Phase

Forehand Lob   *Backhand Lob*

_____ 1. Follow through up naturally   _____
_____ 2. Return to ready position   _____

d   d

Detecting Forehand and Backhand Lobbing Errors

Lobbing is a very physical shot that requires fast footwork and good reflexes. However, by using the correct techniques and avoiding the following errors, you should be able to execute a good lob—and, with practice, perhaps become a very good lobber!

ERROR 🚫

CORRECTION

ERROR	CORRECTION
1. The ball goes off the end.	1. Hold the racket less firmly. Open the racket and lob higher so the incoming ball's speed dissipates into upward motion. Make sure you aren't too close to the table.
2. You're not getting enough topspin on your lobs.	2. Make sure you're grazing the ball at contact. A spinless lob is not nearly as effective as a topspinning one.
3. You're unable to react to smashes.	3. Make sure you aren't too close to the table. Try not to move too soon—wait until your opponent is committed to a direction. Be light on your feet so you can react quickly. The instant your opponent strikes the ball, move!

TOPSPIN DEFENSE

An advanced version of lobbing is called "topspin defense." Topspin defense is a mixture of looping and lobbing. Instead of lobbing the ball high in the air, use a looping motion and try to topspin the ball without letting it get too high—no more than 4 to 6 feet above the net, preferably lower. Because of the flatter trajectory, and because of the topspin, the ball will take a fast hop when it hits the table, with a lower bounce. This will force many mistakes, and a slow opponent might even have to block if caught out of position. Control is more important on this shot than extreme topspin.

SMASHING THE LOB

Some players have very good smashes and yet have great difficulty when faced with a high, spinny lob. On the other hand, many players smash poorly but when faced with a lob have no problem. It's all a matter of correct technique. When your opponent smashes, you will always smash with your forehand. If a ball bounces higher than your head, it can be very difficult to smash it with the backhand, but relatively easy with the forehand. Because the ball is traveling very high, it will take longer to reach your side of the table, thereby giving you more time to prepare for a forehand smash.

There are two common ways to kill a lob. First, there is the regular smash of lob. This is similar to a regular smash but there are differences. The regular smash you learned earlier was geared toward smashing balls that landed below eye level. When the ball goes much higher, as it does in a lob, you have to raise your arms higher. This could throw you off balance if you don't adjust. Also, when you smash a lob, you have more time to put full power into the smash. This is important because a lobber stands far from the table and has more time to return any hit except a hard smash.

Another common way to kill a lob is the smother kill. This is like a regular smash except the ball is taken right off the bounce. (See Step 3, Forehand

Smash.) It's difficult to do consistently but is nearly unreturnable. A smother kill should be done only against a ball that lands short on the table, especially if it has little spin.

Smash Against the Lob

Start by judging exactly where and how deep the ball will land and how much spin it has. Get into position. If you're confident that you have read the ball correctly, stay close to the table and take the ball on the rise. Otherwise, step back and take the ball as it drops.

Reading spin against a lob can be tricky at first. Watch to see if your opponent grazed the ball, or simply hit it straight on. Also, watch to see how the ball curves in flight; if it has spin, it will curve. If the ball has topspin, it will curve down. If it has sidespin, it will curve sideways. Against topspin, aim lower, and be ready for the ball to jump fast when it hits the table. Against sidespin, aim to the side, and be ready for the ball to jump to the side when it hits the table.

Stand sideways, with your right foot back. Shift your weight to the back foot; drop your playing arm and shoulder. Rotate your upper body back (see Figure 11.2a). Then bring your playing arm back up (see Figure 11.2b).

Push off your back foot and drive your upper body forward. Snap your elbow forward. Your playing arm will move in a continuous half-circle up and over your head, and over the contact point (see Figure 11.2c). Your right foot should lift off the ground just before you contact the ball. Contact the ball just above eye level, either on the way up or on the way down. Contact should generally be very flat, but if the ball is near the net, you can add chop or sidespin to your shot to make it harder to return. Follow through naturally, with your body rotating almost 180 degrees (see Figure 11.2d).

Figure 11.2   Keys to Success: Smashing Lobs

Preparation Phase

1. Relax arm ____
2. Judge depth and spin of lob ____
3. Move into position, several feet from table ____
4. Right foot back ____
5. Drop playing arm and shoulder ____

Execution
Phase

Backswing

1. Rotate upper body back ____

b

Forward Swing

1. Push off of back foot ____
2. Raise arm ____
3. Throw upper body into shot ____
4. Right foot lifts up ____
5. Snap arm through ball ____
6. Contact ball on rise below eye level, or just
   above eye level on drop ____

c

Follow-Through
Phase

1. Follow through naturally ____
2. Return to ready position ____

d

Smother Kill Against the Lob

A smother kill is just like a normal forehand, except the ball is taken just after the bounce. However, the timing is far more tricky, so you must make sure to do it just right, or you'll miss it. Watch the ball closely so that you can judge where and how fast it will bounce. A smother kill should usually only be done against a lob that lands very short. Stand close to the table and contact the ball right after it hits the table (see Figure 11.3).

Exhibition Lobs

Try some exhibition lobs with or without a partner: Lob while sitting in a chair, lob with your back turned (turn back at the last minute), smash your own lob (lob high, and run like heck to the other side of the table!) or eat a candy bar while lobbing, throw

Figure 11.3   A smother kill requires accurate timing.

the wrapper over your shoulder and countersmash! Half the trick, however, is getting a partner who can smash accurately. Your partner should smash to a prearranged spot, not too hard, and no smother killing.

Detecting Smashing of Lobs Errors

Smashing lobs is quite different than most other smashes, and many players with great smashes have difficulty in smashing lobs. Check to make sure you aren't making any of the mistakes below, and you should develop an effective smash against lob.

ERROR

CORRECTION

ERROR	CORRECTION
1. The ball goes into the net or off the end.	1. Read the spin and adjust the racket angle.
2. You're not getting enough power.	2. Make sure to push off your back leg, throw your upper body into the shot and snap your arm. Accelerate through the shot.
3. You're inconsistent.	3. Get in position. Don't get too close to the table. Relax your muscles, and watch the ball. Make sure to drop your arm at the start of the stroke or you'll be off balance. Don't smother kill unless the ball lands near the net.

Lobbing Drills

1. Lob Against Bounced Ball

Stand about 15 feet from the table. Drop the ball on the floor so that it bounces to waist height. Lob the ball on the table. Try to put topspin on the lob. The ball should go at least 10 to 15 feet in the air. This is a good way to get the lob form right, without having to react to a smash.

Success Goal = 15 consecutive lobs from a bounced ball, both forehand and backhand

Your Score =

    (#) _____ consecutive forehand lobs

    (#) _____ consecutive backhand lobs

2. Lob Against Smash

Have your partner smash (not too hard at first) to your forehand. Lob the ball. Then do the same with your backhand.

Success Goal = 5 consecutive forehand and 5 consecutive backhand lobs

Your Score =

    (#) _____ consecutive forehand lobs

    (#) _____ consecutive backhand lobs

3. Lob Against Random Smash

Have your partner smash (not too hard at first) randomly to any side. Lob the ball.

Success Goal = 5 consecutive lobs, forehand or backhand

Your Score = (#) _____ consecutive lobs, forehand or backhand

4. Smash Against Lob

Have your partner lob. Smash, going for consistency first and then speed as you get consistent.

Success Goal = 10 consecutive smashes against lob

Your Score = (#) _____ consecutive smashes against lob

5. Lob Game

Play a lob game with the following rules. Your partner spots you 10 points in a game to 21. You start each rally from 15 feet or so from table, and serve a lob. (Just toss the ball up and lob it.) Keep the serve deep! Your partner smashes to forehand over and over, and you lob. Then do the same, with your partner smashing to your backhand. Then repeat, with partner lobbing this time.

Success Goal = Win at least half of the games played

Your Score =
- (#) _____ games won lobbing
- (#) _____ games lost lobbing
- (#) _____ games won smashing
- (#) _____ games lost smashing

6. Smother Kills

Have your partner lob. Smash until the returned lob lands short, then smother kill.

Success Goal = 5 consecutive successful smother kill attempts (not necessarily on consecutive shots)

Your Score = (#) _____ consecutive successful smother kills

7. Countersmash

Have your partner smash to one side while you lob. When you see a chance, countersmash. The most important thing to look for when deciding when to countersmash is whether you're in position or not. Mostly countersmash with forehand.

Success Goal = 10 countersmashes

Your Score = (#) _____ countersmashes

8. Group Lob Game

Get three or more players together. One person is the lobber, one person is the hitter, the rest get in a line. The lobber lobs, and the hitter smashes. If the lobber scores, the next person in line takes the place of the hitter, and the lobber gets one point. If the hitter scores, she becomes the lobber. (You can only score when you're the lobber.) Game is to 11 or 21 points, with everyone competing against everyone else. The lobber has the option of countersmashing, but the countersmash has to win on one shot—if returned, the lobber loses the point immediately. When a lobber successfully countersmashes, the player who lost the point gets a point taken away from his score! This helps reinforce the idea that when smashing against a lob, a player shouldn't give the lobber a chance to countersmash—smash mostly to the backhand.

Success Goal = Win at least one of the games played

Your Score = (#) _____ games won in group lob game

Lobbing
Keys to Success Checklists

Have your instructor or practice partner verify with the Keys to Success checklist (see Figure 11.1) that you're doing both the forehand and backhand lob properly. Have them verify that you're not just "getting it back." Have them pay particular attention to depth and spin of your shot. Also have them use the Keys to Success checklist (see Figure 11.2) to check that you're smashing lobs correctly.

Step 12 Advanced Serves: Really Getting the Initiative

Earlier you were introduced to simple topspin and backspin serves. If you have perfected those serves, it's time to learn more advanced ones. Some of the more popular serves to be explained here are the backhand sidespin serve, the forehand pendulum (also known as the high toss serve), and the backhand fast serve. Also shown are illustrated sequences of other popular serves. These serves are more advanced because they use speed or spin (including sidespin) to increase their effectiveness. Also discussed are the factors that make up a good serve—deception, spin, height, depth, and (for some serves) speed.

WHY ARE GOOD SERVES IMPORTANT?

At this point, you have mastered most aspects of the game, or at least are well on your way to doing so. However, your opponents probably have also, and they're going to do whatever it takes to keep you from using what you've learned. It's pointless having a good loop, for example, if every rally starts off with your opponent attacking and you blocking.

Good serves give you the initiative. Earlier, the four basic serves you learned gave you initiative at that level. However, now you're up against stronger competition (hopefully!) and those serves won't help you so much anymore. Your opponent will probably have serves much better than those you learned earlier; the only way to keep up is to develop your own serves. Not only will they let you take the initiative when you serve, but they will also win you many points outright as your opponent struggles to return them without giving you setups.

To improve your serve, you must improve your deception and placement and increase the spin on the ball while still keeping it very low. First I'll talk about deception.

SERVICE DECEPTION

Deception is achieved by using a semicircular motion. For example, you may start with the racket pointing sideways, and swing first down, then sideways, and then up, all as part of the same swing. If done quickly, it is difficult to tell at which part of the swing contact was made. If done on the downward swing, you get chop. If done while swinging sideways, you get sidespin. If done while swinging up, you get topspin. You can also create sidespin/chop and sidespin/topspin by contacting the ball between the downward and sideways motion or between the sideways and upward motion. With practice, you can learn a variety of serves using semicircular motion, getting a different spin each time by contacting the ball at a different part of the swing. Note that although you have changed the spin, you have not changed the service motion!

To increase deception even more, use a deceptive motion after the serve. Exaggerate your follow-through in a direction other than that at contact. For example, for a chop serve, follow through up, and for a topspin serve, follow through down. Of course, if you do it every time, it becomes predictable. Judge how often you can get away with it. You don't want to let your opponent know you're serving topspin by always following through downward after the serve!

By varying where on the racket you contact the ball, you can also vary the spin. When you serve, not all parts of the racket move at the same speed. The tip usually moves faster than the base of the racket. So by contacting the ball at the tip, you can get heavy spin, and with the same motion, you can get very little spin by contacting the ball at the base. A no-spin serve, such as this, is as effective as a spin serve. Your opponent will have a hard time telling the difference between the two.

Of course, the best way to deceive an opponent is to put so much spin on the ball that the degree of spin becomes hard to read.

SPIN

For maximum spin, you must use both forearm and wrist. Failure to use either cuts down on your spin. You should also contact the ball toward the tip of the racket because it moves faster than the rest of the blade in a circular motion, giving more spin.

Don't think of the serve as a "gentle" shot. The serve can be almost a violent shot, since you want the racket to be moving as fast as possible at contact. At first, you will not be able to control the serve at top speed, so do it slower. Eventually you want to get maximum racket speed at contact, and still just graze the ball while keeping it low.

HEIGHT

An often underrated part of the serve is its height. It is important to keep the ball low at all times. This requires a good touch. Always contact the ball as low to the table as possible, within 6 inches of it. That way it won't bounce as high on the far side. It will also make it easier to serve short.

DEPTH

The last component of a good serve is its depth. There are two types of good serves: short or long.

A short serve should be short enough so that, if given the chance, it would bounce at least twice on the opponent's side of the table. This makes your opponent reach over the table to stroke the ball, making it more difficult to attack. To serve short, make the ball bounce close to the net on your side of the table as softly as possible. If it bounces too close to your endline, it will have to travel too far to the net to stay short. The serve can be made either very short, so that it would bounce several times on the opponent's side of the table, or so that its second bounce would be near the opponent's endline. The first makes him reach way over the table, while the second keeps his target (your side of the table) as far away as possible while still making it difficult to attack.

A deep serve should bounce within 6 inches of the endline. This forces the opponent away from the table and puts his or her target (your side of the table) as far away as possible. A deep serve is easier to attack than a short serve, especially with the forehand, so it should usually be served fast into the backhand to force the opponent to return with the backhand. If your opponent keeps stepping around and using his or her forehand, a sudden serve down the line done very fast will catch your opponent out of position, often with an ace. If your opponent is attacking your deep serves effectively, serve short. If you can't serve short effectively, learn to.

EXECUTING THE BACKHAND SIDE SPIN SERVE

Start facing to the left, with your feet and shoulders at about a 45-degree angle to the table (see Figure 12.1a). Hold the racket loosely in front of you. Toss the ball up between 6 inches and 2 feet. Backswing about 1-1/2 feet behind the ball, above and to the left of it. During the backswing, open the racket and cock your wrist back, so the racket points backward and slightly up. The racket should be tilted back at about 45 degrees to the floor (see Figure 12.1b).

Now swing forward using your forearm, as if you were going to do a chop serve. Contact the back bottom side of the ball slightly to the right when it drops to just above table level (see Figure 12.1c). This will give sidespin chop. At contact, snap your wrist and just graze the ball. Your elbow should snap upward, pulling the racket up (see Figure 12.1d). For deception, use a semicircular motion, going first down, then up.

To get sidespin topspin, delay contact until the racket is moving upward along the semicircular motion, and then graze the back of the ball, slightly to the right, with the racket going forward and up. To get pure sidespin, contact the back of the ball slightly to the right between the topspin and chop serve contact points.

By using this semicircular forward swing, you can now serve three serves (and all variations in between) with the same motion. The only difference is when contact is made, and if you learn to do the service motion very quickly, it will be difficult for your opponent to tell when it was done. So practice doing it faster and faster, whipping the racket down and then up so fast there's no way the opponent will see contact! And, of course, by moving your forearm faster and snapping your wrist more, you'll get more and more spin.

Figure 12.1   *Keys to Success:*
Backhand Sidespin Serve

**Preparation
Phase**

1. Stand in backhand corner ____
2. Face left (feet and shoulders at about a
   45-degree angle to the table) ____
3. Ball in palm ____
4. Racket held slightly behind ball ____
5. Racket open ____
6. Relax arm ____

a

**Execution
Phase**

Backswing

1. Bring racket to left side, behind future contact
   point ____
2. Toss ball 6 inches to 2 feet high ____
3. Cock wrist back ____

b

Forward Swing

1. Pull forward with right shoulder ____
2. Accelerate racket with elbow ____
3. Racket goes through semi-circular
   motion ____
4. Contact
   a. Back bottom of ball slightly to the right
      during downward part of swing for
      sidespin/backspin ____
   b. Back of ball slightly to the right during
      bottom part of swing for pure
      sidespin ____
   c. Back of ball slightly to the right during
      upward part of swing for sidespin/
      topspin ____
5. Snap wrist at contact ____
6. Contact ball just above table height ____
7. Graze ball near tip of racket ____

c

**Follow-Through
Phase**

1. Pull racket up vigorously ____
2. Return to ready position ____

EXECUTING THE FOREHAND PENDULUM SERVE

This is probably the most popular serve at the higher levels. At first, you will do it with a relatively low toss, perhaps 1 or 2 feet high. After you have learned it that way, you should learn to do it with a high toss, tossing the ball up to 10 feet in the air.

For this serve, you'll have to change your grip. Rotate the top of the blade away from you about 30 degrees. Hold the racket between your thumb and index finger. Slide your index finger, which usually lies along the bottom of the blade's surface, more onto the surface of the blade. Your index finger should make about a 45-degree angle to the bottom of the blade (see Figure 12.2). (Some point their index finger almost straight down.) Put your thumb onto the blade, with the soft part of the thumb partly resting on the sponge opposite your index finger. Hold the racket loosely. By holding the racket this way, you can rotate it with your wrist at least 180 degrees. Practice snapping the wrist a few times, accelerating as fast as you can.

Now stand to the left of your backhand corner, facing to the right so that your body is perpendicular to the endline. Hold the racket in front of you with the blade roughly parallel to the floor (see Figure 12.3a).

Now bring the racket back and away from the body with your elbow. Your arm should straighten somewhat, pointing mostly back. The racket should still be parallel to the floor and pointing

Figure 12.2   The forehand pendulum serve grip.

almost straight back. Cock your wrist back during the backswing; this will point the racket a little to the side. For extra deception, hide the racket with your body until just before the forward swing (see Figure 12.3b).

Toss the ball straight up about 1 or 2 feet. Keep the ball within a foot of your body and just behind the endline.

During the forward swing, the playing elbow should stay almost motionless. Moving it forward will actually reduce the amount of spin produced by reducing elbow snap. Racket speed should come mostly from rotating the arm around the elbow and from the wrist. Bring the racket forward and toward your body as rapidly as possible in a semicircular motion. Graze the back bottom left side of the ball, snapping your wrist at contact (see Figure 12.3c). Elbow should still be high, racket open. This will give a sidespin/chop serve.

After contact, follow through up with a semicircular motion, with the racket ending up almost against the stomach (see Figure 12.3d).

To get sidespin/topspin, contact the ball later in the swing. As the racket reaches the bottom of the swing, bring it up and in toward your body. Graze the left back side of the ball in an upward and sideways motion. By contacting the left back of the ball at the bottom of the swing with the racket going sideways, you'll get a pure sidespin.

Again, as with the backhand serve, the speed of the racket is important: The faster it's moving, the more spin and deception you'll get. For even more deception, follow through down or off to the side at the end of the stroke, keeping the upward part of the semicircular motion to a minimum.

Figure 12.3   Keys to Success: Forehand Pendulum Serve

Preparation Phase

1. Stand in backhand corner ____
2. Face mostly to the right ____
3. Ball in palm ____
4. Adjust grip, wrist swings free ____
5. Racket held just behind ball ____
6. Racket and ball low to table ____
7. Racket parallel to floor ____
8. Relax arm ____

a

Execution Phase

Backswing

1. Rotate body backward ____
2. Bring racket back and away from body with elbow ____
3. Hide racket with body ____
4. Toss ball 1 or 2 feet high ____
5. Cock wrist back ____

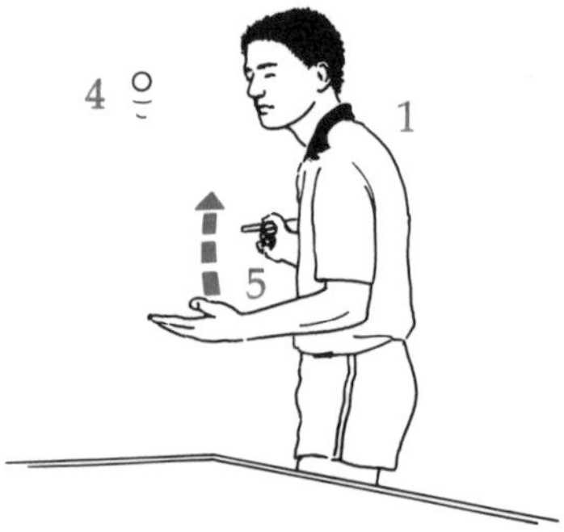

b

Forward Swing

1. Rotate upper body forward ____
2. Accelerate arm forward ____
3. Racket goes through semi-circular motion ____
4. Racket approaches ball from far side ____
5. Contact
   a. Back bottom of ball slightly to the left during downward part of swing for sidespin/backspin ____
   b. Back of ball slightly to the left during bottom part of swing for pure sidespin ____
   c. Back of ball slightly to the left during upward part of swing for sidespin/topspin ____
6. Snap wrist at contact ____
7. Contact ball low to table ____
8. Contact near body ____
9. Graze ball near tip of racket ____

c

Follow-Through Phase

1. Pull racket up vigorously ____
2. Follow through down or to the side for extra deception ____
3. Return to ready position ____

d

EXECUTING THE HIGH TOSS SERVE

One of the most popular serves at the higher levels is the high toss serve. Before attempting it, you should first learn the forehand pendulum serve—the high toss serve is merely an advanced version of this. A high toss can also be used with other serves, but the pendulum serve seems most effective with this toss.

For this serve, the ball is tossed 5 to 10 feet (and sometimes even more!) into the air. When the ball comes down, it's falling faster than with a lower toss. This will convert to extra spin on contacting your racket, if you graze the ball. Also, since the ball is traveling so much faster than normal, it's harder for the opponent to see contact, making the serve more deceptive. This also makes the serve far more difficult to master; you're trying to graze a rapidly moving object. The best way to practice any serve is to get a bucket of balls and serve, pick them up, and serve again.

EXECUTING THE BACKHAND FAST SERVE

You learned to do a backhand topspin serve earlier. But just getting it on the table isn't enough. The serves taught so far are all spin serves. Now you're going to learn a fast serve. The key to a fast serve is, of course, its speed. You don't want to give your opponent time to react! The ball should bounce on the very end of the table, as close to the endline as possible.

Start as if you were doing the backhand topspin serve, which you learned in Step 4. Swing straight into the ball as if you were doing a backhand drive. The ball should hit your side of the table close to your endline to give it as much time to drop on the other side as possible. Contact the ball within an inch or so of the table surface.

At contact, you can either do a slight grazing motion to give it some topspin or serve it "flat." A flat serve has no spin and is actually more effective than a spin serve when done very fast. To make the flat serve even flatter, put a slight amount of backspin on it to compensate for the ball's rolling motion when it hits the table. That way it will be truly spinless and hard to handle.

Fast serves are usually done to the backhand, like deep spin serves. However, if your opponent is stepping around his backhand too soon, you can ace him with a fast serve to his forehand.

OTHER SERVES

Service is sometimes called the "trick" part of table tennis. You should master a few established serves, but you should also invent your own. Watch other players for ideas. You might try learning a forehand serve with the racket tip up. It can be done with the racket going either left to right (more common; see Figure 12.4, a and b) or right to left.

You might try using different grips, such as the Seemiller grip, which enables you to do a "windshield wiper" serve, with racket tip up and going in either direction (see Figure 12.5, a and b).

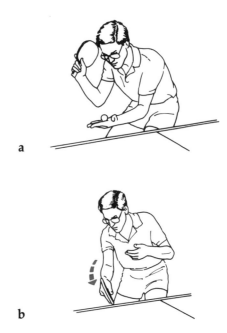

a

b

Figure 12.4   Add variety to your forehand serve with the racket tip up.

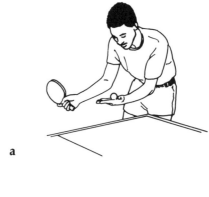

a

b

Figure 12.5   The Seemiller grip serve.

There are an incredible number of variations. Just remember to use circular motion of some sort on all spin serves. You can also experiment with different types of fast, deep serves (different placements, spin, etc.). Also experiment with different contact points on the racket, mixing up no-spin and spin. A great variation of all the spin serves explained so far is to simply contact the ball near the handle; this will make a no-spin serve look like it has spin.

Try to develop two types of serves: those that stop your opponent's attack and set you up for your own, and those that force an opponent into an immediate error. Generally, favor the first type, and use the second as a surprise. If you overuse the second type, a good player will adjust and you won't be able to use that serve anymore.

Detecting Service Errors

The three biggest problems beginners face when trying advanced serves is getting enough spin, keeping the ball low, and stopping their short serves from going long. Look over the error and correction section and make sure you aren't making any of these common mistakes.

ERROR 🚫

CORRECTION

ERROR	CORRECTION
1. You're not getting enough spin.	1. Make sure you're grazing the ball. Accelerate at contact and snap your wrist.
2. Your opponent attacks your serve.	2. Make sure the serve is low to the net. A short serve (especially with backspin) is usually harder to attack than a deep serve.
3. Your arm doesn't accelerate.	3. Relax your arm. Make sure your backswing is long enough to generate racket velocity.
4. Your short serves are going long.	4. Make the first bounce close to the net and low. Turn racket speed into spin, not forward motion, by grazing the ball lightly.

Advanced Service Drills

For the following drills, you'll need either a bucket of balls or a partner to return your serve. Unless you are instructed otherwise, catch the return and serve again.

1. Spin Serves

Do each variation of your four favorite spin serves. Go for as much spin as possible, even if it means you're inconsistent at first.

Success Goal = 20 consecutive each of four favorite spin serves

Your Score =

    (#) _____ consecutive spin serve #1

    (#) _____ consecutive spin serve #2

    (#) _____ consecutive spin serve #3

    (#) _____ consecutive spin serve #4

2. Fast Serves

Serve your fast backhand serve (or any other fast serve variation that you prefer). Serve it as fast as possible, even if it means you're inconsistent at first. The purpose of this serve is to catch your opponent off guard, and you can't do that unless the serve is very fast.

Success Goal = 15 consecutive fast serves

Your Score = (#) _____ consecutive fast serves

3. Short Serves

Serve short with spin, first with backspin, then with sidespin. You may have to take off some of the spin to make sure the ball stays short, but not too much, and eventually you'll be able to serve with full spin and still keep it short. The advantage to serving short is that it keeps your opponent from attacking effectively (especially loopers) while usually setting you up for an attack—especially a loop attack. Most players return serves deep, setting up your loop, and many players build their games around this.

Success Goal = 10 consecutive short backspin serves, 10 consecutive short sidespin serves

Your Score =

    (#) _____ consecutive short backspin serves

    (#) _____ consecutive short sidespin serves

4. High Toss Practice

Toss the ball up about 6 feet over your head. Without actually trying to catch the ball, try to make the ball hit your hand on the way down (don't actually serve at this point). When you have mastered this, you can go on to practicing high toss serves.

Success Goal = 5 consecutive balls hit your hand

Your Score = (#) _____ consecutive balls hit hand

5. Accuracy Game

Play a game similar to the accuracy game taught in Step 4. Put four targets (such as a lid to a jar) on the opponent's side of the table, one near each of the two corners, one in the middle backhand area, one in the middle forehand area. Serve fast topspin twice consecutively, aiming for the corner targets, then serve two sidespin serves consecutively, aiming for the two closer targets. Do this in a circuit. See who can hit the most targets in the circuit in a given amount of repetitions. Games are to 11 points.

Success Goal = Hit more targets than anyone else at least once

Your Score = (#) _____ times hit most targets

6. Serve Variations

Play regular games to 21 points with two variations. Each server chooses at least five different serves to use throughout the game. Each time the ball is served, the player must use a serve that is different from the last serve. If the receiver misses the serve outright, the server gets two points.

Success Goal = Use 5 different serves and try to win at least 1 game

Your Score =
    (#) _____ serves used
    (#) _____ games won

7. Serve and Attack Game

Play games where you practice serve and attack. Spot your partner 5 points. You serve every time, mixing up the serves. Your partner should receive passively, either by pushing or driving relatively slowly. You attack the return, and play out the point. Games are to 21 points. This drill allows the server to practice attacking, while the receiver learns to handle the server's attack. The 5-point spot is to make up for the server's advantage.

Success Goal = Win at least half the games played

Your Score = (#) _____ games won, (#) _____ games lost

8. Receive Attack Game

Play games where you practice attacking the serve. Your partner serves every time, and you attack deep serves with a loop while flipping short serves, backhand or forehand. Your partner spots you 5 points; games are to 21 points.

Success Goal = Win at least half the games played

Your Score = (#) _____ games won, (#) _____ games lost

9. Serve and Smash Game

Play a game where the server must always serve and smash, ending the point on the first shot after the serve. The receiver can return the serve with any kind of shot. The receiver is trying to keep the server from smashing and scoring. Whenever the server fails to make a point-winning smash on the first shot, the receiver becomes the server. There's one catch—players can only score points when they're serving! Games are to 11 points.

Success Goal = Win at least half the games played

Your Score = (#) _____ games won, (#) _____ games lost

Advanced Serves
Keys to Success Checklists

To spin the ball well when serving, you must remember several cues: loosen the arm, accelerate the racket into the ball, snap the wrist, and graze the ball. Ask your coach, instructor, or practice partner to watch you and verify that you are performing the advanced serves properly. Are your serves legal? Can you do both topspin and backspin with the same motion?

Have your evaluator use the Keys to Success checklists (see Figures 12.1 and 12.3), and also listen to the contact—a good grazing contact is almost soundless. Keep in mind that most of the sound comes from the ball sinking through the sponge and hitting the wood. Finally, make sure you can do all the variations of spins. Many players think they can serve topspin, backspin, or sidespin, but in reality all three turn out to be nearly the same.

Step 13   Playing Styles and Rallying Tactics

Playing styles and rallying tactics go together because your playing style dictates how you want to rally. As you learn your playing style, you learn the proper rallying tactics for your style, and when you play against a specific style, you'll use specific rallying tactics that work against that style.

There is no such thing as a pure style. Everybody uses a little bit of several styles, and usually a lot of one. Loopers are called loopers because they loop a lot, but they generally block or hit on occasion as well. Similarly, there are no rules carved in granite on how to play specific styles; everyone plays a little different and has different strengths and weaknesses. However, you can divide most players into some combination of the following:

- Loopers
- Hitters
- Counterdrivers
- Blockers
- Choppers
- Lobbers
- Combination racket users
- Doubles players—all combinations of the preceding styles, except now there are *two* different styles to take into account!

You also have to take into account the various types of grips and rubbers available. That's a lot of combinations! Without a lot of thought, there is no way you can make the most of your game. That's why it is so important to know both your playing style and your opponent's, and to know what tactics you should use.

However, the following guidelines should help in either playing with or playing against a given playing style. If the rule says serve short to a looper, try it! But if your opponent flips winner after winner against it, be flexible: Try something else. Ultimately, it's up to you to match your strengths against your opponent's weaknesses so that you end up with 21 points first.

While reading this section, look at both sides of the fence. Recognize your own style and how others should play you. Then learn how to combat that with your own personal inventory of shots.

LOOPERS

Loopers come in many varieties. Some like to loop kill the first ball while others will loop 10 in a row to win 1 point. Some run all over the court looping only with the forehand while others cut down on the footwork by backhand looping as well. Some let the ball drop below table level before lifting it in a sweeping but often defensive topspin while others practically take the ball as it bounces on the table. And then there are those who combine looping with some other shot such as chopping or hitting. There are very few set rules for loopers.

As a looper, you want to loop as early in the rally as possible; serve with that in mind. Then keep looping until the rally is over or you get an easy kill—which you may loop kill.

A loop that lands short is easy to kill or block at a wide angle if it's taken quickly off the bounce. Therefore, a looper should loop deep unless the opponent is too slow to react quickly to a short one. Most players are weaker blocking on one side, often the forehand, and most loops should go to that side. Try to get into rallies that let you loop over and over with your forehand into the opponent's weaker blocking side. An alternate strategy is to loop over and over into the stronger side, then looping an easy winner through the weak side. This will work if the stronger blocking side is more consistent than fast, giving you the opportunity to keep looping. A favorite strategy of loopers is to loop over and over with the forehand from the backhand corner, usually into the opponent's deep backhand court.

When an opening appears, loop kill to either side or the middle. Don't always loop to the corners. Many players are weak blocking from the middle due to indecision as to whether to use the forehand or backhand. But others are strong there, and weak covering the wide corners. Find out the weakness and go there.

Note that if you loop to a corner, the opponent can block back at a wide angle. By going to the middle, you take away the extreme angles. It does give your opponent an angle down both sides, but if you keep your loop deep, your opponent won't be able to get a good angle, and you'll probably be able to keep looping forehands.

Another thing to take into account is variation. Most players will get into a rhythm against your loop if you always do it the same. Loop at all speeds—fast, medium, and slow. A slow loop is surprisingly hard to block effectively—in fact, it's usually either attacked hard or returned very poorly.

Loopers have three basic weaknesses:

- They can't loop a ball that doesn't bounce past the endline on the first bounce.
- They must take longer strokes that slow them down somewhat.
- Because they use some power to put spin on the ball, some shots lose speed.

What if you're playing against a looper? The most obvious way to beat one is to not let him or her loop. Serve short and push chop-serves back short, and what is a looper to do? A smart one will flip the ball and try to loop the next one, but if you serve and push low (and short), the flip will be soft and you'll be able to attack it.

Of course, if the looper does flip or serve topspin, take advantage of Weakness #2: the longer stroke. Flip the topspin serve aggressively or attack the flip quickly to force your opponent back from the table to have time to loop, taking away much of the loop's effectiveness. And once the looper is away from the table, he'll have difficulty looping winners—not only do you have more time to react to the shot, but Weakness #3 comes in: Speed is sacrificed for spin. You can plain outlast the looper who can't get the ball past you, as long as you can handle the topspin.

Of course, some loopers look like they just got out of a powerlifting meet and if they lose power to spin, it's not noticeable. Against these Herculean players you must be careful not to give an easy shot. Let them loop 100-mile-per-hour zingers. If they don't hit, you win! If they do, well, work on making stronger shots yourself so they can't keep on zipping in shots. You might also use their own speed against them. If you block a fast loop, it'll probably go back so fast your opponent won't be able to react to it!

A one-sided looper rushes all over the court trying to use a forehand. Don't make the mistake of going to the backhand over and over. A looper's strongest loop is often the forehand from the backhand corner. Instead, go to the wide forehand first, then come back to the backhand. Your opponent will probably have to return the second shot with a weaker backhand. Attack it.

If the looper seems a little slow, go wide to the backhand, which forces either a weaker backhand or a step around. Then a quick block to the looper's wide forehand will often win the point or set you up to end it. Even if it doesn't, a quick return to the wide backhand will make your opponent use a backhand.

A two-sided looper stands in the middle of the table and loops both backhands and forehands. The key here is to find the opponent's weaker side and play to it, usually the backhand. (Or, of course, just don't let him or her loop!) Move your opponent in and out—backhand loopers are especially vulnerable to that movement. A hard block followed by a soft one is usually more effective than two hard ones in a row because it breaks the looper's rhythm. Also, note that most two-sided loopers are relatively weak in the middle against a hard block. Unlike a forehand looper, a two-sided looper has to decide which side to loop with. Remember that a two-sided looper's middle is wherever his or her playing elbow is.

A consistent looper just keeps looping until you miss or return an easy shot. Loopers usually loop from both sides, but not always. You must move a looper around as much as possible, both side to side and in and out. Although you hope a looper will miss, don't count on it. Usually you'll have to earn the point by attacking a weak loop or ending the point before your opponent loops. Force a looper off the table with your own aggressive attack, whether it be blocking, hitting, or your own looping. If you see a winner, go for it. If not, keep moving your opponent, attacking whenever you can. But watch out for spin. If you make too many mistakes against it, you'll lose. This is true against all loopers.

General Tactics

For loopers:

- Loop as early in the rally as possible.
- Keep loops deep.
- Loop to wide corners and opponent's middle.
- Vary speed, spin, and placement of loops.

Against loopers:

- Keep serves and pushes short.
- Attack first.
- Hit shots quick off the bounce.
- Move opponent in and out.

HITTERS

In general, there are three types of hitters. There are pure forehand hitters, often pips-out penholders. There are two-sided hitters, hitting winners from both sides. And there are hitters who loop to set up their smash.

There are two common tactical mistakes hitters tend to make. Some are too tentative and don't let themselves go for the shot. Hitters must be somewhat reckless, or they'll find themselves constantly trying to decide what to smash. There's no time for that! All hitters must accept the fact that sometimes you must go for a dumb shot to make sure you don't miss an opportunity to smash. But, surprisingly, many of these "dumb" shots actually go in!

The other common mistake is just the opposite—trying to hit too much. A hitter should hit right from the start of the rally, and also use some judgment. Rather than hit the first ball for a winner every time, why not hit an aggressive drive first and smash the next ball, which might be easier?

A hitter wins by quickness and speed. Accordingly, hitters should stay close to the table, take the ball quickly off the bounce, and hit the ball as fast as they can consistently do so.

A hitter should find out which side an opponent is weaker on and go to that side over and over, always looking for a ball to put away. Hitters should go to the strong side only when they can make a strong shot or when the opponent is out of position.

A hitter who mostly likes to hit with one side will have to be especially reckless. The longer the rally goes on, the more opportunities for shots to be made from the weaker side and the more likely there will be a mistake. Go for the shot!

Two-sided hitters can be more picky and play longer rallies because they are a threat to hit from both sides. Although two-sided hitters should end the point as quickly as possible, they're under less pressure to do so. Two-sided hitters can hit strong drives (instead of smashing) knowing that there is no worry about a return to a weaker side—there isn't any.

Hitters with a good loop have a tremendous advantage if they are able to get both shots going. They should loop the ball as deep and spinny as they can, but not too fast. A slower, spinnier loop will set up the smash more while a faster one usually is blocked back faster, giving you little time to get into position to smash.

A hitter is probably the most mentally demanding style to play against. No matter what you do, it seems hitters are able to hit winners. Yet keep in mind that a hitter's shots often miss. Don't be intimidated—it's the quickest way to lose, and hitters thrive on it. Hitters simply cannot win if they don't get enough good balls to hit. It's up to you to deprive them of that. All-out forehand hitters have few shots to set up their smash. But they make up for it in the simplicity of their game. They've often grooved their one winning shot so much that no one thing you can do compares to it.

The key to beating a hitter is versatility. Hitters can only beat you one way; you can beat them a dozen ways. Find the way that works. You might force them to go backhand to backhand with you, or loop everything, or just mix up the spins. You can keep changing until you find something that works; the hitter can't. Take advantage of it.

If a hitter gets into a groove, the game's over. After all, the hitter has mastered the most powerful shot in the game; if you can't stop it, you're going to lose. Keep the hitter out of the groove by constantly changing your shots, making your opponent hit different types of balls over and over.

A smash has a much smaller margin for error than just about any other shot. Keep that in mind at all times. A hitter might hit five winners in a row and then miss five in a row, so never give up.

Hitters like to start off the point with a quick serve and smash. They'll often serve fast and deep, trying to catch you off guard with an easy winner. Be ready for it. Attack the serve and hitters will get very uncomfortable. Often they'll still smash, but as long as they must go for risky smashes, you're in control. Watch to see if they step around the backhand corner too much. If so, return the fast serve wide to the forehand with a quick drive or block.

You can also throw hitters off by moving them around. Like loopers, they're often strongest hitting forehands out of the backhand corner. In general, you should either try to pin them upon the backhand or you should go side to side, making them hit as many backhands and moving forehands as possible. Because they stand so close to the table, hitters often cannot react to a quick block to the wide forehand after stepping around. Of course, the problem here is that the forehand shot from the backhand corner may already have been a winner, or at least strong enough to keep you from making a good return! (And if they do get to that wide forehand ball—watch out!)

Since hitters want to hit everything, if you attack first (especially with loops), they are forced to either go for low percentage hitting, or to abandon their game. The best defense is often a good offense.

Two-sided hitters can hit from both sides, so moving them around pays off less. However, like two-sided loopers, they're often weak in the middle where they must decide which side to hit with. But only go there aggressively. A weak shot to the middle gives a hitter an easy winner.

Find a two-sided hitter's weaker side and go there until you find an opening to the other side. Combat the hitter's speed with your own drives, and try to be more consistent than your opponent. Play to the hitter's weaker hitting side.

Since two-sided hitters are trying to hit from both sides, they often are erratic because they don't have time to set up their shots on both sides. They often hit hard but cannot all-out smash until an easy ball comes, because they're trying to do so much on both sides. Also, most two-sided hitters are slower on their feet; they don't need to step around often. Try to take advantage of this whenever they move out of position. Two-sided hitters are often weak against backspin because they usually specialize in hitting topspin.

Looper/hitters use the loop to set up the smash. Usually they'll loop backspin and smash topspin. Because they only need to smash against one type of spin, their smashes are often more consistent. And unlike an all-out hitter, they have a loop to set up the smash.

The basic weakness of looper/hitters is that they're trying to do too many aggressive shots. It's very hard to learn to both hit and loop well, and even harder to get both in a groove at the same time. Looping is basically a lifting shot while hitting is a forward shot, and trying to perfect both modes at the same time can create havoc with your timing. This leads to many missed shots. Only the fact that they smash one type of ball (topspin) saves them.

Most looper/hitters loop softly and then smash. Attack the soft loop. If you just block it passively, you're playing right into their game. From the hitter's point of view, a slow loop has more spin than the fast loop and forces more setups, while giving more time to get into position for the smash. Make hitters loop more aggressively by attacking the slow loop. They'll have less time to react to the next shot, they'll make more mistakes on the loop, and they'll have to concentrate more on the loop and less on the smash, leading to more missed smashes. There's nothing looper/hitters hate more than someone who can attack their loops.

General Tactics

For hitters:

- Find balance between recklessness and tentativeness.
- Try to get a smash into a groove.
- Stay close to table and hit shots quick off the bounce.
- End points quickly.

Against hitters:

- Don't be intimidated by smashes or recklessness.
- Play high percentage shots.
- Attack first.

- Vary shots.
- Attack weaker side.

COUNTERDRIVERS

Counterdrivers like to stand in the middle of the table and just stroke back whatever you hit to them. They usually take everything at the top of the bounce and smash given the first opportunity, especially on the forehand side. They seemingly can counter your best shots and go on doing so all day. It's a simple game, with placement, consistency, and speed of drives the most important elements.

To be a counterdriver your basic strategy is to drive balls mostly to your opponent's weaker side. If the backhand is weak, your basic goal is to keep the opponent from stepping around and using a forehand. If the weaker side is the forehand, hit hard enough to it so your opponent cannot smash the return. If the opponent tees off on your shots, you have to pick up speed. If you start missing, slow down. And always be on the lookout for balls to smash.

The weakness of a counterdriver's shots is that they are neither quick, fast, or spinny. Just as counterdrivers can drive back whatever you throw at them, you should be able to do the same. It usually comes down to whether your attack is more consistent than the counterdrive.

To play against a counterdriver, concentrate your attack at the weaker side and to the middle. Most counterdrivers are very strong from the corners, although they are often weaker or softer on one side. Take your time attacking. Pick your shots, and make sure that the winners that you go for are just that. It takes sharp judgment, but you must avoid going for the wrong winners, a temptation when playing counterdrivers. Remember—if they can't put the ball past you, you're under no pressure to force the attack.

On the other hand, don't take too long. Counterdrivers will be more consistent than you at their own game, and if you rally too long, you risk too many careless mistakes. However, you might counter just until you see a chance to smash, either forehand or backhand. Another way to play the counterdriver is to end the point before the chance to counterdrive. The key here is good serves and a good attack. Against aggressive players, it is dangerous to overanticipate a third-ball kill when serving—a good receive catches you off guard and the receiver ends the point instead. But because a counterdriver is usually less of a threat on the attack, you can play a flexible all-out attack. Look to put the first ball away, but if the shot isn't there, fall back on rallying and looking for a better shot.

General Tactics

For counterdrivers:

- Be consistent.
- Counter mostly to opponent's weaker side.
- Build up a countering rhythm.
- Force countering rallies early.

Against counterdrivers:

- Be patient and pick shots.
- Attack middle and weaker side.
- Don't try to beat counterdrivers at their own game.
- Use topspin and backspin to break up rhythm.

BLOCKERS

Blockers are similar to counterdrivers except that they contact the ball right after it hits the table. They tend to be as consistent as a counterdriver but are constantly putting pressure on you by rushing you. This means that they can even go to your stronger side knowing that you won't have time to go for a strong shot.

A blocker can either block every ball quickly to the opponent's weaker side, exploiting it to the fullest, or block side to side, making the opponent move about and hit on the run. A blocker has to be ready to smash when a weak ball comes, or all an opponent has to do is keep the ball in play. Blockers have to anticipate weak returns so as to have time to smash, or even designate one side (usually the forehand) as the side to smash whenever possible. Many players combine a backhand blocking/forehand smashing game. A quick backhand block will often set up the forehand smash.

The weakness of blockers is their own quickness. To take the ball so quickly they must stand right at the table. They have little time to decide what shot to use, and so even if you make a weak shot, they'll often just block it. This is why a blocker needs to anticipate weak balls to be ready to kill them. Blockers will also make a lot of mistakes by their own attempts to be quick.

Some blockers are very strong in the middle but weak to the corners, where they have to move their racket farther. Others are the reverse, being weak in the middle because they have to decide which side to block with. Find out early in a match which type you're playing. There are basically two types of blockers: aggressive ones and consistent ones. Aggressive ones want to block the ball hard and quick, forcing you away from the table and into

mistakes. If they succeed in forcing you away from the table, they have extra time to watch your incoming shot and so they become quicker. Worse, it gives them time to go for more smashes.

What you want to do against aggressive blockers is attack so aggressively that they make mistakes trying to block aggressively or are forced to slow down their blocks so that they can keep their own shots on the table. Once they've slowed down their blocks you have time to really go on the attack.

A consistent blocker tries to keep the ball in play until you make a mistake. He or she can be like a brick wall, getting everything back until you almost drop from exhaustion. His or her shots are usually passive, but they're quick enough to prevent you from teeing off on them. And when you do, they often keep coming back!

Consistent blockers' weakness is their own passiveness. They put so much effort into getting everything back that they can't do much else. You can slow down your own shots, giving yourself more time to set up for the next shot. Take your time, look for the right shot, and then end the point fast at their weakest point.

Don't make the mistake of letting a consistent blocker get into a rhythm. Don't always attack at the same pace. Surprisingly, a blocker usually has more trouble blocking slow, spinny loops than faster ones. The spin on a slow loop grabs the racket more and jumps out more. The blocker will often pop them up or miss them outright. The slowness of your own shot makes his shot slower, and the slowness of both shots gives you more time to get into position for your own more aggressive strokes. A fast loop just comes back faster and should be used with discretion until you can put it past your opponent.

Many blockers like to push to your wide backhand over and over, waiting for you to step around with your forehand. Then they give you a quick block to the wide forehand. (It's almost a style by itself, sort of a pusher/blocker style.) You have five ways of combatting this. First, you can attack with your backhand, and never go out of position at all. A backhand loop is ideal for this. Second, you can loop the push itself for a winner. You have to judge whether you can do this consistently enough. Third, you can be quick enough to get to that block to your wide forehand. Fourth, if the blocker has a passive forehand, you can push to his forehand to take away the angle into your backhand, and attack his return. Or fifth, you can use your forehand but loop slow and deep. The very slowness of your shot gives you time to get back into position, and the depth keeps the blocker from contacting it too soon.

General Tactics

For blockers:

- Hit shots quick off the bounce.
- Block to the weaker side.
- Always be ready to smash.
- Vary pace and placement.

Against blockers:

- Attack all parts of the table.
- Be patient and pick shots—not too aggressive.
- Use slow, spinny loops.
- Keep ball deep.

CHOPPERS

Choppers are defensive players who win mostly on your mistakes. They go 15 feet or so away from the table and return each of your aggressive topspin shots with backspin, making it difficult to attack effectively.

A chopper doesn't simply get the ball back. Chopping is probably the most tactical of games because to win a point, choppers must fool their opponents into making a mistake in some way. This can be done by outlasting them, by heavy spin, by spin variation, by pick hitting, or by keeping every ball low until they get frustrated and go for reckless shots.

If you're a chopper, you have to decide which of the above tactics will work best against whoever you're playing. If the player is mistake-prone or not very powerful, concentrate on keeping the ball in play until he misses. Change the spins only when you see an easy chance to.

If an attacker has trouble with heavy chop, give it to him. If an attacker has trouble reading spin, change the spin over and over, even if it means popping up a few balls. (If an attacker has no trouble hitting them, he or she's then reading the spin and you should change strategies.)

As a chopper, you should put pressure on your opponent by attacking whenever possible. Because you pick which shots you'll attack (called "pick hitting") instead of attacking over and over like an attacker you should make the most of them. Go for immediate winners when you do attack—if you were as effective attacking for several shots in a row you'd be an attacker, not a chopper. It's the surprise of a chopper's attack that makes it effective; after one or two shots, the surprise wears off.

Some players are emotionally incapable of playing a steady chopper. Even if they have the shots to win, a chopper can beat them by playing on their impatience. The chopper keeps the ball as low as possible and watches them swat shots all over the court!

A chopper should be aware of the expedite rule. (See explanation in Step 10.) Some players will push with a chopper for 15 minutes and then win in the end. To end a game before the 15-minute time limit you might have to take the attack. Once in the expedite rule, of course, you have to attack whenever you serve. Keep in mind that you don't have to rush the attack, even in expedite. Very few rallies actually go 13 shots, so pick your shots carefully. It's better to hit a winner on the 10th shot than miss the 1st shot.

The natural weakness of choppers is that they must rely on your mistakes. They can pick hit when they see the chance, but basically they must score most of their points on your misreading their spin or just making a careless mistake. In theory, you should be able to dominate against a chopper—after all, if you can't attack a given ball, you can push it and attack the next one instead. Any time you're not sure of the spin you can do this. So how does a chopper win?

From an attacker's point of view, an attacker is in control of the rallies when they attack. But from the chopper's point of view, the chopper is in control. Against a low chop or push, an attacker can only attack so hard and still be consistent. If the chopper can chop that shot back effectively, he or she's in control.

Of course, the attacker could just push. But choppers are usually better at pushing and can do so forever. They can also catch the attacker off guard by attacking when they see the chance; the attacker can't do the same because the chopper is expecting it.

In general, if a chopper can return your best drives without giving you a high ball, you're going to lose. But there are ways to make your drives more effective.

A common misconception about playing choppers is that you have to overpower them. Nothing could be further from the truth. If you can beat choppers on pure power, then you would beat them by even more points if you choose your shots more carefully.

After a chopper has made one return of a strong drive, he or she'll probably return the same drive over and over again. Choppers can adjust to just about anything if they see it enough. What does give them trouble is change. Changing the spin, speed, direction, depth, or even the arc of the ball can create havoc to their timing and lead to misses and high returns.

Choppers are strongest at the corners unless you can force them out of position and ace them to a wide angle. They're weakest in the middle, where they must decide whether to chop with the forehand or the backhand and then get into position for a proper stroke.

When playing a chopper, constantly change depth and direction. Loop (or hit) one deep, then go short and spinny. Draw a chopper in close to the table and then attack hard before he or she can react to it. Force a chopper away from the table and then drop shot the ball, followed by another hard attack. Have patience, but when the shot is there, take it. If you have trouble reading the spin, push one or attack it soft. Don't attack to the corners too much—concentrate on the chopper's weaker middle. Put as much pressure on a chopper as you can in order to elicit mistakes. Often the mistakes aren't obvious. An outright miss or a high ball are obvious mistakes, but a chopper might also chop too short. A chop that lands midway between the net and the endline is usually easy to loop kill or smash (for a hitter) even if it's low. Take advantage of all mistakes, limit yours, and you'll probably win.

Another way to play choppers is to push with them very patiently, looking for a good ball to attack. Push 10 balls, then wham! They won't know when you're going to attack and might get stuck too close to the table to return your shot. You can even push until the expedite rule takes effect and then you'll have an advantage, because an aggressive player can win the point quickly under expedite better than most choppers can.

One common mistake against choppers is to go for too many drop shots (as opposed to regular pushes). A drop shot is an excellent way to win a point if you can catch your opponent too far from the table, but it's risky. There are three reasons for this. First, a drop shot is a very delicate shot and is easy to miss. Second, it's easy to pop a drop shot up, giving the chopper an easy ball to pick hit. Third, it's difficult to do a good drop shot against a deep chop; if the ball lands any shorter it should be easy to attack and so you wouldn't want to drop shot. (Unless, of course, it lands so short that it would bounce twice.) Another mistake is to drop shot when you aren't sure of the spin. The worst thing you can do when you don't read the spin is to drop shot because you'll invariably either put the ball in the net or pop it up. Choppers are notoriously good at swatting in high drop shots, even on the run. If you aren't sure of the spin, just use a normal push or attack softly. If you are sure of the spin, and the chopper is far from the table, then by all means drop shot.

General Tactics

For choppers:

- Be patient and confident.
- Vary degree of backspin.
- Always be ready to attack, especially on serve.
- End points quickly when attacking.
- Take every shot seriously, even pushes.

Against choppers:

- Attack middle.
- Move in and out.
- Be patient.
- Vary all shots.
- Don't overdo drop shots.

LOBBERS

Most players use the lob only as a variation or desperation shot. But some players use it over and over, and if they find you have trouble with it, they'll use it even more. Lobbers have to be strong on both sides or their opponent will simply smash to the weak side. Most lobbers are stronger on the forehand side; they can counterattack easier on that side, so it's a good idea when lobbing to lob to the hitter's forehand side, tempting your opponent into smashing the easy way, crosscourt to your forehand. But if your opponent is smart, he or she won't fall for it, and you'll mostly lob with your backhand (which might be what you want, if that's your stronger lobbing side). The most important thing to remember when lobbing is depth. As long as your lob goes deep, you're still in the point. A short lob can be smashed at such a wide angle that there's nothing you can do to get it back.

When lobbing, don't just throw the ball in the air. Try to put topspin and sidespin on the ball to force mistakes. Vary the height of the lob—sometimes lob high, other times lower. Short players especially will have trouble with high lobs.

A lobber should always be on the lookout for a chance to get back into the point. Countersmash every chance you can. If the smash is weak, you might even chop it back.

There are two ways to hit a lob. A smother kill is most effective if it hits, least effective if it misses. You have to judge for yourself. Some players smother kill all lobs, others never do it. A good balance is to smother kill only against lobs that land short, near the net, close to your target.

Regardless of how you hit the lob you should follow one fundamental rule when playing lobbers: Smash mostly to the backhand. (Of course, there's an exception to this rule out there somewhere and you'll no doubt encounter it in your next match.) The forehand lob is usually spinnier, and it's far easier to counterattack with the forehand than the backhand. So just smash to the backhand over and over until you force either a miss or a weak return. When the weak ball comes (one that is short or less spinny) go to the forehand only if you can smash an ace or at least force a leaping return. Why take chances? When in doubt, keep going to the backhand.

If your opponent isn't a great threat to countersmash, go for the middle. Many lobbers have trouble lobbing from that spot.

When the ball lands short, end the point. You can angle the ball to either side. Unless your opponent can anticipate (or guess) which side you're going to, you should be able to put it past him. Don't decide which side to go to until your opponent has committed to one side. If there's no commitment, then both wings should be open. (And with both sides being equal, you should go to the backhand, just in case.)

Often you'll be faced with a relatively easy lob to smash. Make sure to use good form; shots like this are often far trickier than they look.

You should rarely drop shot against the lob. If the ball is deep, an effective drop shot is nearly impossible, and if the ball is short you should be able to put it away. A drop shot against a lobber usually just lets your opponent back into the point. One exception to this rule is when your opponent has gotten into such a rhythm that you cannot smash past your opponent in the rally. A drop shot might be effective just to throw off your opponent's timing, but don't do it too often.

General Tactics

For lobbers:

- Keep ball deep and spinny.
- Lob to spot diagonally opposite stronger lobbing side.
- Look for balls to counterattack.
- Avoid lobbing except when forced.

Against lobbers:

- Smash mostly to backhand side unless ready to end point on one shot.
- Consider smashing at the middle.
- Against a good lobber, smother kill short lobs.
- Use good form no matter how easy a shot looks.
- Rarely drop shot.

COMBINATION RACKET USERS

One of the first problems you'll face when you begin playing in USTTA-sanctioned tournaments is "junk rubber." The two types of rubber usually classed as junk are long pips and antispin. Hard rubber and short pips-out sponge are also considered junk by some players. Basically, since most players use inverted sponge, anything else is different and therefore junk.

Junk rubber is called such by many players not because it is of lesser quality, but because the racket's characteristics are very different from most types you will face. They can be difficult to play against unless you regularly play opponents who use the stuff. However, it must be noted that as hard as it can be to play well against them, it's equally hard to learn to use them effectively.

Before the different color rule came into effect in the early 1980s, many players used different surfaces on each side of the racket, and by flipping the racket, they could make it difficult for opponents to tell which side they were hitting with. This led to many unforced errors (due to the different playing characteristics of the different surfaces) and many cries of "foul," with some justification. But the color rule made it illegal to have both surfaces the same color: Now you always know what surface is being used, by seeing the different colors, so there's no excuse for making mistakes against the so-called junk rubbers. At the start of the match, find out what color each surface is. It's just a matter of learning to play each type. If you lose to a player because you can't handle long pips, it's just as much a loss as if you lost to someone because you couldn't handle the loop.

Antispin and Hard Rubber

Antispin rubber was first introduced in the early 1970s. It's actually a variation of inverted sponge. The major characteristic of antispin is its slick surface. When the ball contacts it, it slides, and spin barely affects it. This makes it easy to handle spinny shots, and it's primarily used to aid in the return of loops and serves. Most antispin rubbers have a very dead sponge underneath, which makes it easy to return hard drives. With its slick surface and dead sponge, an antispin player can seemingly return anything!

Hard rubber is primarily like antispin except that it puts slightly more spin on the ball and reacts to spin slightly more. Hard rubber is simply a sheet of pimpled rubber with no sponge underneath—exactly like pips-out sponge without the sponge. It's usually (but not always) slightly faster than antispin.

Most hard rubbers are easier to attack with than antispin. These two surfaces have primarily the same characteristics.

A ball hit with antispin or hard rubber has less spin than a ball hit with inverted or pips-out sponge. Players often react as if there were more spin on the ball than there actually is. If you play against antispin or hard rubber, you'll learn to react to its different characteristics.

The weakness of antispin or hard rubber is that their returns are generally weak and easy to attack. They take spin off the return, so all their returns are relatively spinless and easy to handle. They're also more difficult to attack against topspin, although backspin can be attacked effectively. This makes antispin and hard rubber very limited surfaces unless used in conjunction with a different type of surface, usually a grippy inverted; this racket can be flipped to use either surface. The important thing to remember is that antispin and hard rubber cannot generate much spin, and they usually deaden what spin there was on the ball. Also, balls hit off antispin or hard rubber tend to land shorter on the table, because these surfaces are slower than most surfaces.

Antispin and hard rubber are primarily used by two styles, choppers and blockers. Choppers use them to return loops consistently, sometimes winning by getting so many balls back that the opponent tires and gets impatient. But the returns are easy to attack by a good player, and there are fewer and fewer choppers using antispin or hard rubber these days. Those that do use antispin or hard rubber almost invariably have inverted on the other side, and most flip their racket to confuse their opponent. Most choppers find that long pips are more effective in conjunction with inverted sponge.

Blockers sometimes use antispin to return serves and block loops and drives. The antispin makes it easy to push serves back short, stopping an attack, and its slick surface makes spinny serves easy to return. It's also easy to block a loop with antispin, but the return is easy to attack if anticipated. Most blockers who use antispin use the Seemiller grip so that they can use either inverted or antispin on both sides at all times. They'll push the serve back short with the antispin, flip back to inverted to play out the point, and then suddenly flip back to antispin to block a ball short, often catching the opponent off guard.

General Tactics

For antispin or hard rubber users:

- Use antispin and hard rubber sparingly, if possible.

- Use to return serves (especially short ones) and drop balls short.
- Attack backspin.
- Flip racket—use combination racket.

Against antispin or hard rubber:

- Recognize lack of spin.
- Play into antispin and hard rubber and attack return.
- Stay closer to table.
- Serve deep.

Long Pips

The long pips surface is a type of pips-out sponge with pips that are much longer and thinner than conventional pips. This lets the pips bend at contact with the ball, which creates an interesting effect. If the ball has spin on it, it continues to rotate in the same direction. But because the direction of the ball has changed, the spin has changed. A topspin ball continues to spin in the same way but because its orientation has changed (it's now going toward your opponent), it now has backspin. Imagine a topspin ball coming at you, with the top of it rotating toward you. If you hit it back without changing the rotation, the top will still be rotating toward you, or away from the opponent. This makes it a backspin return. Likewise, backspin can be returned as topspin.

If you were to block a topspin ball back with conventional surfaces, your return would have a light topspin. The same block with long pips will have backspin. Even if you use a topspin stroke with long pips, against a topspin you'll return the ball with either a backspin or at most a very light topspin. However, if you attack backspin you'll get topspin because the ball is already rotating in that direction, but the topspin will still be less than with other surfaces.

If you chop a topspin with a long pips surface, you'll return all the spin as backspin. Against a spinny loop you'll give back a very spinny chop, spinnier than is usually possible with any other surface. Against a light topspin, however, all you can return is a light backspin. And against backspin, a long pips push will either return a light topspin or at most a very light backspin. (Weak players constantly hit this off the end, expecting more backspin; good players go for winners against it.) Note that the longer and thinner the pips, the greater the long pips effect. No sponge or thin sponge also increases it. Basically, conventional surfaces put their own spin on the ball. Antispin takes the spin off. But the long pips surface returns and reverses the spin, something most players are not used to. The amount of spin you receive from long pips depends more on the spin on your previous shot than on the long pips stroke itself. This is what makes the long pips surface the hardest surface to play against. But don't despair. It's also one of the hardest to control.

Against a ball with no spin, a long pips user can only return no spin or at most a very light spin. This makes it easy to attack against, at least for one shot. To keep attacking effectively, you must understand the way the long pips surface returns different shots and be prepared for the spinless return (or the reversal of spin in other shots) regardless of the stroke used by the long pips user. It can completely throw off your reflexes because the spins of the returns go contrary to what you're used to. But they are predictable and you should be able to adjust to them.

The long pips surface is difficult to attack with, especially against topspin. Against chop, it's easier to attack with, but the effectiveness of the attack is mostly due to the weirdness of the playing characteristics of the surface. Most balls attacked with a long pips surface with a topspin stroke will have less spin than expected and so are often returned into the net. But once you have adjusted to the lack of spin of a long pips surface attack, it should give you no more trouble. (Against a very heavy push, a topspin shot made with a long pips surface will have considerable spin, however.)

Two features of the long pips surface that make it attractive to choppers are the ease in returning loops and drives and the heavy backspin returns against loops. Next to antispin (or possibly hard rubber) the long pips surface is the easiest surface to chop a loop back with because the spin doesn't take on it. And since loopers get all their spin back, they have great difficulty in continuing an attack. Thus the long pips surface is especially effective when chopping against loops. The only problem is that if the looper pushes your chop return, you might have to push. If you do so with long pips, your return not only will have little spin and be easy to attack but will also be difficult to keep low. A backspin ball travels in a straight line and so spends a good portion of its time at just above net height, if done correctly. This gives you a large margin for error—all you have to do is make sure it crosses the net while at that height. But a spinless push with long pips arcs more, spending only a short time at the proper height, and is difficult to keep low. Only a good touch and a lot of practice will enable you to do so. One solution is to have inverted sponge on one side and learn to flip. Even if you can't flip fast enough to always use the side you want for every shot, at least your opponent can't get into a rhythm, expecting a weak return every time you push.

Some blockers use long pips without any sponge underneath. This makes it easy to block topspin and somewhat easy to attack backspin. The long pips surface's effect is at its most extreme with no sponge. But you'll always be at the mercy of your opponent with this combination. It will be very difficult to push with, and almost impossible to attack a topspin, even a light one. Yet some players have found success this way, usually with the long pips on the backhand and an attacking forehand. They'll attack backspin to keep you off guard but basically rely on the long pips to keep the ball in play until you make a mistake. Note that if you take up this style, against topspin you shouldn't just block with the long pips. At contact, you should chop down on the ball, sort of a chop-block. This gives your opponent maximum backspin and maximum difficulty. Also note that the problem with pushing can be partially solved by staying close to the table, as blockers do, and pushing right off the bounce. This enables you to be as close to your target as possible, which makes it easier to keep the ball low. It also rushes your opponent.

General Tactics

For long pips:

- Use mostly to chop, block, and attack underspin.
- Use combination racket and flip, especially when pushing.

Against long pips:

- Be prepared to get your own spin returned.
- Serve deep to long pips.
- Deep no-spin balls are difficult to return with long pips.
- Push quick and deep to long pips, and attack return.
- Don't loop over and over to long pips.
- Stay closer to the table.

Short Pips

This surface is similar to inverted except that it gives less spin on each shot.

Balls struck by short pips will have little spin, but they will come out as expected—that is, a topspin stroke produces predictable topspin and a chop stroke produces predictable backspin. The difficulty in playing short pips is that there is always less spin than the inverted sheets you're probably more used to playing, leading to many balls going into the net or off the end (not only because you misread the spin but also due to overcompensation). You will simply have to adjust to them.

The short pips surface (also called pips-out sponge) is especially useful in attacking spin shots. But keep in mind that although pips-out players can attack spin shots well, they cannot produce as much spin as players using inverted surfaces. You should take advantage of this. They cannot loop, push, or serve with as much spin. They should have more trouble against heavy inverted spins more than inverted players have against a pips-out player's lighter spins.

Note that every legal surface except inverted has been covered in this section on junk rubbers. Yet there was a time when inverted was the junk. Until the 1950s, nearly everyone used hard rubber, and even in the 1960s there were as many pips-out and hard rubber players as inverted ones. When players were first faced with the inverted surfaces, there was an outcry against the surfaces for being "different." It's only in the last 25 years that most tournament players have gone to inverted sponge. In most of Asia, there are still nearly as many pips-out players as inverted, and the 1985 and 1987 World Champion, Jiang Jialiang of China, used pips-out sponge.

General Tactics

For short pips:

- Develop smash.
- Stay close to table and hit shots quickly off bounce.
- Don't be afraid to hit against any type of spin.
- End point quickly.

Against short pips:

- Push heavy and deep.
- Use heavy topspin shots.
- Recognize lack of spin on returns.

DOUBLES

The rules for doubles are similar to singles. The three major differences are (1) players must always serve from the right side crosscourt, (2) partners alternate shots, and (3) the order of service. The order of serving is set at the start of the match, with the team order changing after every game. For example, if players A and B play Y and Z, the first game order might be A serving to Y, who serves to B, who serves to Z, who serves to A, and so on (see Figure 13.1, a-d). In the second game, the order would be A to Z to B to Y to A. (If A or B served first in the first game, then Y or Z serves first in the

second game. Either player on the team can serve first as long as the correct team is serving.)

Tactics in doubles can be complex. It's like singles except now you have four styles to worry about instead of just two. The points are usually shorter, and serve and receive become more important. Placement also becomes more important; it's easy to win points by catching an opponent out of position. Generally, the more aggressive team wins because one hot player can carry a team.

A left-hand and right-hand pair (lefty/righty) combination has an inherent advantage, assuming each player favors the forehand. They can stand in their respective backhand corners, their natural ready position, without getting in each other's way. A lefty/righty combination can play almost all forehand shots while two right-handers (or two left-handers) have to move quickly to keep up a forehand attack. However, although lefty/righty teams do dominate many tournaments, many same-handed teams have become very good, including some world champion teams. It just takes good footwork.

The simplest footwork method is for each player to take the shot, and then move backward and slightly off to the side. This takes each player out of the partner's way and keeps each player in position for the next shot. If a player were to simply go off to the side, the opponents would quickly hit to that side, and the player would be in his or her partner's way. Even if the player's partner makes the shot, he or she'll be way out of position for the next one, which will undoubtedly be to the far side and out of reach.

Because your opponent knows where you are serving (into the opponent's forehand corner), deep serves are rarely used in doubles except as a surprise. They're too easy to attack. Most teams favor short chop or no-spin serves, or short topspin/ sidespin serves. The problem with short topspin/ sidespin serves is that they can be flipped to a wide angle very easily and if placed well can cause the serving team to get in each other's way. Chop serves are harder to flip aggressively.

Receivers should set up to receive with their strongest side, usually the forehand. If they are stronger on the backhand, then they should receive backhand, even though the serve is going to the forehand corner. When receiving in doubles, be ready to attack (especially by looping) any deep serve. Vary the receive against short serves, but don't push deep too often or your partner will be faced with a strong attack. Mix in flips and short pushes with occasional deep pushes.

Doubles rallies are similar to singles rallies except

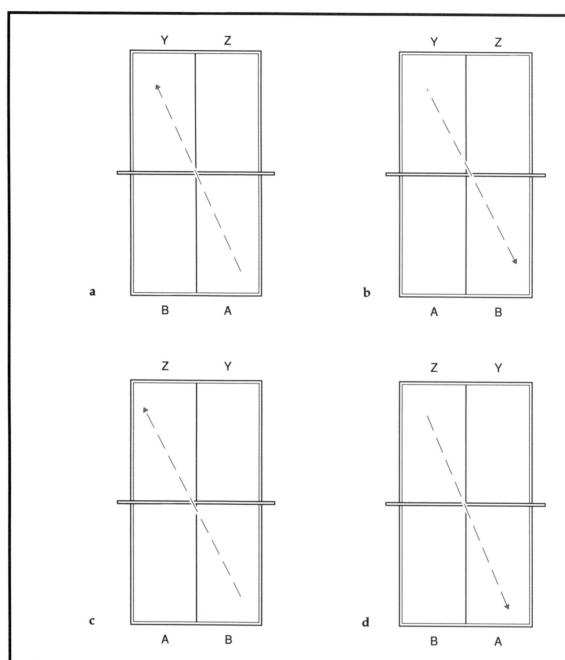

Figure 13.1   In doubles serving use the following order: A serves to Y (a), Y serves to B (b), B serves to Z (c), and Z serves to A (d).

that each player has to take into account the partner's playing style and abilities. For example, a defensive player might be perfectly at home letting the other team attack, but if his or her partner is an attacker, then there might be mixed signals as to how to handle the opponent's attack.

The most important rallying tactic in doubles is to hit the ball back at the opponent who hit the ball before the opponent has a chance to get out of his or her partner's way.

General Tactics:

- Serve short.
- Attack first.
- Receive with stronger side.
- Team up left-handed and right-handed partners when possible.
- Play as a team, not as an individual.
- Return shots back at person who hit to you.

Playing Styles and Rallying Tactics Drills

1. Personal Styles and Strategies

Play a practice match with your partner, two out of three games to 21 points. Afterward, analyze the match and discuss it with your opponent. Write out the following:

    a. Your best rallying shots during the match
    b. Your weakest rallying shots during the match
    c. How you can improve your weakest rallying shots

Success Goal = Name your 3 best rallying shots and 3 weakest rallying shots; decide how you can improve your weakest rallying shots

Your Score = Your answers to the questions

    a. Best rallying shots:

    _____

    _____

    _____

    b. Weakest rallying shots:

    _____

    _____

    _____

    c. Improvement goals:

    _____

    _____

    _____

2. *Playing Style*

Based on what you have learned so far, and from all previous match experience, describe your playing style in a few sentences. Some things to decide: Are you an offensive or defensive player? Are you better at the start of the rally against backspin or topspin? Do you favor attacking by hitting or looping? Keep in mind that table tennis is not a game where everything is black and white; you can be both a looper and a hitter, for example.

Success Goal = Ability to pinpoint your personal playing style

Your Score = Write out your thoughts

_____

_____

_____

3. *General Tactics*

Think about each style of play and racket surface mentioned in this step. Then think about how you play. How would you, with your playing style, play against each different style? It's often better to think about these things, and figure them out for yourself (even if you get it wrong at first) than it is for someone to simply tell you what to do. After all, no two players play the same. If you want to become a top player, you've got to become the top authority in the world on how you personally play. Reread this step if you have any trouble deciding how to play any of the styles below.

Success Goal = Identify at least two tactics against each style

Your Score =

   (#) _____   tactics against a looper

   (#) _____   tactics against a hitter

   (#) _____   tactics against a counterdriver

   (#) _____   tactics against a blocker

   (#) _____   tactics against a chopper

   (#) _____   tactics against a lobber

   (#) _____   tactics against antispin or hard rubber

   (#) _____   tactics against long pips

   (#) _____   tactics against short pips

4. *Playing Different Styles*

Find players about your level who could be classified as loopers, hitters, counterdrivers, blockers, choppers, lobbers, or some combination of these styles. Plan out a strategy for playing them, and play games with them.

Success Goal = Win at least half the games played

Your Score =

   (#) _____ games won, (#) _____ games lost against looper

   (#) _____ games won, (#) _____ games lost against hitter

   (#) _____ games won, (#) _____ games lost against counterdriver

   (#) _____ games won, (#) _____ games lost against blocker

   (#) _____ games won, (#) _____ games lost against chopper

   (#) _____ games won, (#) _____ games lost against lobber

5. *Combination Rackets*

Find players about your skill level who use antispin, long pips, short pips, or hard rubber. Or have your partner use these surfaces so you can practice against them. Play games, making sure you understand what you have to do differently against each surface.

Success Goal = Win at least half the games played

Your Score =

   (#) _____ games won, (#) _____ games lost against antispin

   (#) _____ games won, (#) _____ games lost against long pips

   (#) _____ games won, (#) _____ games lost against short pips

   (#) _____ games won, (#) _____ games lost against hard rubber

6. *Centerline Weakness*

You've been told that most players are weak in the middle. Now you get to see for yourself! Have your partner hit everything at your elbow. You decide whether to use a forehand or backhand, and drive the ball back to your partner's backhand. If you use one side too often (for example, too many backhands), your partner should aim a little to the other side. This drill should illustrate the value of ball placement.

Success Goal = 15 consecutive drives against balls hit to middle

Your Score = (#) _____ consecutive drives against balls hit to the middle

7. Doubles

You and your partner play a practice match, two out of three to 21 points, against another doubles team. During the match, concentrate on two items: (1) hit the ball back to the player who hit it at you, and (2) make sure to move mostly backward to get out of the way of your partner, not off to the side. See if the first strategy gets the opposing players in each other's way, and if the second tactic keeps you and your partner out of each other's way.

Success Goal = Win at least half of the games played.

Your Score = (#) _____ games won, (#) _____ games lost

Step 14 Advanced Service and Receive Strategy

To play your best, you must learn the proper tactics for your personal playing style. For example, if you're a hitter, you wouldn't want to be serving the types of serves a looper would use! All players are different, and although there are many "golden rules," there are always top players who routinely break them with success. It comes down to knowing which ones you can break and when. That cannot be taught here—only experience and intelligent thinking can do that.

SERVICE STRATEGY

The type of serves you'll use depends on your strengths and weaknesses. For example, if you're weak against backspin you wouldn't want to serve backspin; a smart opponent will simply push them all back! You'd probably serve topspin. (Of course, if your opponent is a chopper, you're in trouble!)

When preparing to serve, watch your opponent. See how he or she sets up. Does your opponent stand way off in the backhand corner? Your opponent probably wants to return with a forehand. A few fast serves to your opponent's wide forehand corner might make your opponent set up more in the middle, and then you can serve into your opponent's backhand. You can ask yourself dozens of questions like this. Does you opponent seem to be getting ready to attack the serve or just get it back? How has your opponent returned your serves in the past? Most important, how do you want to follow up your serve? This is what should be going through your mind as you prepare to serve. It's before you serve that you must do your thinking—once the rally begins, it's too late.

Most players develop certain surprise serves that can be used to win a point outright but are risky if used too often. A good example of this would be a sudden fast down the line serve to an opponent's forehand, catching your opponent off guard and winning the point outright. The problem with serves like this is that if the opponent is not caught off guard, these types of serves are often easy to attack. If the fast down the line serve doesn't win the point outright, the return will probably be an aggressive topspin shot, and the server is already on the defensive. So don't rely too much on this type of serve.

You shouldn't make a habit of using these surprise serves every time the score is close, for example. You might have one or two that you hold back until you really need it, but it's best to space these serves out over the course of a game, and then the score might not ever reach deuce. Examples of surprise serves are sudden fast serves, very short serves after serving long many times in a row, a serve that looks like it has a lot of spin but really has no spin, or a serve with a jerky motion or exaggerated follow-through to disguise the spin.

Serves can be divided into two categories: deep and short. Each is strong against certain types of players and weak against others. They will each allow your opponent only certain types of returns.

Deep Serves

Deep serves (also called long serves) are ideal for hitters, blockers, and counterdrivers. They will set you up to hit or block, and if that's your style, you should use them frequently. Other styles shouldn't use them as frequently. If you're a looper, the serve usually won't set you up for a loop, so you should use a different serve. However, if your opponent returns deep serves passively, by all means use them.

A fast deep serve is best done to the wide backhand corner, as fast and as deep as possible. You should vary the spin on it, but flat serves, as discussed earlier, are usually very effective when serving fast. Try not to telegraph your intentions—surprise is important.

Although top players can get full spin on the ball and keep it short, that can be difficult. Rather than take some spin off the ball to keep it short, it's often better to go for full spin and let the ball go deep.

Serving deep is also effective in backing players off the table, keeping them from hitting the next shot too quickly off the bounce. Deep serves also force opponents to return the ball from as far away from their target as possible (your side of the table), thereby forcing mistakes. Deep serves also cut off the wide angles on the return.

When using deep spin serves, remember that your opponent has more time to react and move into position to return the serve, and a good player will often attack it with the forehand. Deep spin serves usually aren't effective against a good looper, but if your opponent has trouble attacking the serve or is too slow to cover the wide forehand (after looping with the forehand from the backhand corner), then deep spin serves to the wide backhand are about the best serves to use.

When serving deep sidespins, note that a spin that breaks away from a receiver is usually more difficult to return than one that breaks in to the receiver. This means that a forehand pendulum (or high toss) serve, which breaks to the receiver's left, is usually more effective served to the backhand than a backhand sidespin serve would be, and vice versa. (The same goes for short serves.) Don't overuse this, however—learn to use both types of sidespins to both sides.

By serving to the wide backhand, you can keep most players from looping. If they do step around and use a forehand from the backhand corner, they'll be out of position, and a good block to the forehand will often win the point. However, if your opponent is fast enough to step around and still cover the wide forehand, you should probably use another serve. If your opponent is anticipating your serve and stepping around too soon, a fast serve to the wide forehand will win a quick point and prevent your opponent from moving too soon next time. In general, don't serve deep too often or your opponent will get used to it. If your opponent starts attacking the serve hard with a backhand drive, it's time to try another serve!

Tactical Reasons for Using Deep Serves:

- To set up smash
- To back opponent off table
- To force opponents to contact ball at a distance from their target (your side of table)
- To allow full spin on serves
- To cut off angles on return

Short Serves

A short serve is more difficult to attack than a deep serve, and most top players serve mostly short. Unless your opponent has a good flip (or a good short push against a short chop serve), a short serve will set you up for an attack.

Short serves are used by almost any style of play. They're most effective at stopping loopers from looping. (Because the vast majority of top players loop, this is very important.) Loopers especially like to serve short to set up their loops.

Short topspin or sidespin serves are usually returned similarly, so they are covered together. A sidespin serve will tend to force your opponent to

return the ball to the side, but a good player will adjust, so you can't count on it. However, a sidespin is important because it makes the timing difficult for the receiver. Note that when a player has to reach in over the table to return a short serve to the forehand, the natural racket angle is to go crosscourt. If you give your opponent a sidespin that makes the ball go even more crosscourt (such as a backhand sidespin) you will increase the return difficulty more than using a sidespin going the other way. The same goes for a short serve to the backhand.

A short serve is a good way to bring a player in over the table. Opponents may then have trouble with your follow-up shot, if aggressive—they'll be too close to the table to react. They might also be in an awkward position if they're caught off guard by the short serve and have to reach for the ball (instead of stepping in).

Although you should vary your placement, a short serve is often most effective to the forehand side. It's more awkward to return a short ball with the forehand than with the backhand. The disadvantage is that the opponent can then flip the ball wide to the forehand, forcing you out of position. The same, of course, is true of a short serve to the backhand, except that here the angle is into the backhand, which is easy to handle but takes away your forehand attack. If your serve is being flipped to wide angles, try serving to the middle—it takes away the extreme angles and makes your opponent decide whether to return with a forehand or a backhand.

Short topspin or sidespin serves will nearly always be returned long, usually by a flip. You don't have to worry too much about them being returned short by most players, and of course they can't be looped. A good attacker can serve and then just wait for the deep return to attack. But if your opponent is flipping the serve well, you might have to change serves, probably to a short chop.

A short chop serve can be pushed back short or long, or it can be flipped. If you have a good loop, a short chop serve will set you up over and over to loop against many players who simply push it back deep. Of course, as you play better players, more of them will either push it short or flip it. If you mix in chop and no-spin serves, your opponent will have a hard time adjusting to both. (A very low no-spin serve is surprisingly hard to push or flip effectively.)

A short push against your short chop serve will take away your serve advantage unless you move quickly and flip it. But a good flip against your serve gives your opponent an advantage, so you should try not to let him do it effectively. Keep the serve very low and an aggressive flip return becomes difficult. Chop serves, especially heavy ones, are more difficult to flip than sidespin or topspin ones and should be used if the opponent is flipping well. In that case, you might even consider serving deep.

Tactical Reasons for Using Short Serves:

- To stop opponent from attacking, especially with loops
- To draw a player in close to the table
- To force opponent to reach for the ball

RECEIVE TACTICS

How you return serves depends on your playing style, especially against a deep serve. Obviously, an attacker wants to attack the serve or at least set up to attack the next ball, while a defensive player will return the serve more conservatively. However, regardless of how you plan to return the serve, your opponent has an advantage when serving. If you can break even on your opponent's serve, you'll win for sure. If you average 2 out of 5 points on your opponent's serve, it will probably be a close match.

The most important things to consider are the spin on the serve and the depth. When receiving you should divide sidespins into two types of sidespins: those that break away from you and those that break into you (see Figure 14.1). A typical backhand sidespin serve will break into you if served to your backhand, but break away from you if served to your forehand side. In both cases the spin is the same, and the ball breaks the same way—it simply is served to the opposite side of your body, so the orientation changes.

If a serve is breaking into you, you'll have to contact the outside of the ball—the far side of the back of the ball. If the serve is breaking away from

you, you'll have to contact inside the ball—the inside back of the ball. These two adjustments will make the ball go in the direction you're aiming. It's generally far easier to return a ball that is breaking into you (where you contact on outside of ball) than away from you (where you contact on inside of ball).

Returning Deep Serves

Unless you're a chopper, there's one rule of thumb when returning deep serves: Attack! It doesn't matter whether you attack by hitting or looping, but you must attack. The reason is simple. You're hitting the ball from farther away than you would against a short serve. This gives your opponent more time to react to your receive. If you return passively, your opponent can just tap-dance into position, take a big windup, and WHAMMO! Point's over.

Because it's so important to attack deep serves, it's fortunate that they're easier to attack than short serves. If they weren't easy to attack, everyone would serve deep. The table isn't in the way, and you have more time to react to the ball, so there's no excuse for not attacking a deep serve (unless you don't do it for tactical purposes, or if you're a chopper).

Generally, if the serve isn't too fast, you want to attack the deep serve with your forehand. If you can loop, this is your chance. There's nothing like a good loop to take away a server's advantage. You can even stand off to the backhand side some, looking for chances to use a forehand loop return. Of course, don't stand too far to the side, or you might watch a service ace to your wide forehand. You might want to backhand loop deep serves to the backhand to save yourself the stepping around.

If you can't loop the serve, then drive it, either forehand or backhand. Then get set to smash, counterdrive, or block, whatever your style is. If the serve is fast and deep, use the speed of the ball to counterdrive it.

Tactics Against Deep Serves:

- Attack!
- Loop if possible.
- Against fast serve, use speed to return ball quickly.

Returning Short Serves

There are three ways to return a short serve. You can push it long, you can push it short, or you can flip it. If the serve has topspin, the most common

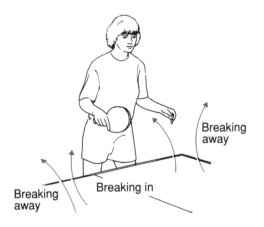

Figure 14.1 When receiving, divide sidespins into two types, depending upon your midline.

Breaking away

Breaking in

Breaking away

receive is to flip it. You can also learn to "chop block" the ball. Some top players can even chop block a short topspin or sidespin serve back short, similar to a short push. A chop block is simply a block where you chop down at contact to create backspin.

Against chop, the simplest return is a long push. At the lower levels, it's the most common and most effective return, but at the higher levels it's used mostly as a variation. The problem is that it gives your opponent an easy chance to loop or hit. It almost always gives the server the initiative. The advantage, of course, is that it's easy to do, so you won't be giving away points on missed returns. Some players, even good ones, have trouble with a low, heavy push, and even those that are good against it can be caught off guard if you throw it at them now and then. Also, sometimes your opponent is just too slow to step around the backhand and attack against it. Or he might be a defensive player. In either case, all you need to do is push deep to the backhand (use a fast or spin push) and you're safe.

One of the most effective returns of serves against short chop serves is a short push. It keeps your opponent from looping and, if kept low, is difficult to flip well. Done properly, it takes away the server's advantage. It's the most common receive at the highest levels against a short chop serve. The dis-

advantage, of course, is that it requires far more touch than a long push, and you'll make more mistakes. Unless you're a very good blocker, a short push is extremely important.

A more aggressive receive is the flip. It can be done against any type of short serve. A good flip is a must for everyone. It allows you to attack the short serve (or a short push) and take the initiative from the server in one shot. Of course, it's even more risky than a short push, and the penalty for trying to get the initiative on the opponent's serve is that you will give some points away if you flip too aggressively and miss. You have to judge how often to flip. Done too often, the opponent gets used to it and might even attack it back. It's best to vary your receive, using all three receives against short chop serves, and also vary the placement and speed of your flip versus short topspin or sidespin serves. And keep in mind that the very threat of a flip is often enough to keep your opponent from attacking a more passive receive effectively. He has to guard against your attack and can't anticipate your receive.

Tactics Against Short Serves:

- Push suddenly to wide angle.
- Push short.
- Flip at wide angles.

Service and Receive Strategy Drills

1. Setup Serves

What serves will set you up for your best attacking shots?

Success Goal = List at least 3 types of serves that set you up for your best attacking shots

Your Score = (#) _____ serves listed that will set you up for your best attacking shots

    a. _____

    b. _____

    c. _____

2. *Serve and Attack Game*

Play games with your partner where you use only the three serves you chose in Drill 1. Your goal is not only to win the point, but to do so by attacking after each serve, if possible. In a real match situation, you wouldn't want to be so predictable, but here you're familiarizing yourself and practicing against all the possible returns against your favorite serves.

Success Goal = Win at least half the games you play with your favorite serves

Your Score = (#) _____ games won with your favorite serve

3. *Surprise Serves*

What serves do you have that will often win you the point outright, or give you an easy winner, by surprising or catching your opponent off guard?

Success Goal = List at least 2 surprise serves

Your Score = (#) _____ surprise serves listed

   a. _____

   b. _____

4. *Surprise Serves Games*

Play games with the score starting out at deuce, 20-20. (Remember—you have to win by two.) The server should try to win the point with a surprise serve of some sort.

Success Goal = Win at least half the games played

Your Score = (#) _____ games won, (#) _____ games lost

5. *Receive Strategy*

Ask a partner to randomly serve a variety of serves to you. Identify at least two types of receives that you find effective against each serve. Reread this step if you don't remember your options!

Success Goal = Identify at least 2 types of receives against each type of serve

Your Score =

(#) _____ receives against a deep side/topspin serve to forehand

(#) _____ receives against a deep backspin serve to forehand

(#) _____ receives against a deep side/topspin serve to backhand

(#) _____ receives against a deep backspin serve to the backhand

(#) _____ receives against a short side/topspin serve to forehand

(#) _____ receives against a short backspin serve to forehand

(#) _____ receives against a short side/topspin serve to backhand

(#) _____ receives against a short backspin serve to backhand

6. *Receive Strengths and Weaknesses*

Play a match with a partner. Answer the following questions:

a. What types of serves are you strong against?
b. What types of serves are you weak against?

Success Goal = Name at least 2 serves that you're strong against and 2 that you're weak against; decide why you are weak against certain serves and take measures to improve

Your Score =

(#) _____ serves that you are strong against

(#) _____ serves that you are weak against

(#) _____ serves that you are weak against, but understand the reason why, and so will improve

The Physical and Mental Game

Many people think of table tennis as a very passive recreational sport requiring little more than the ability to keep the ball in play. To a certain degree, they're right. That's all a beginner does. But once you get into real table tennis, you discover it is something else. The better you get, the more physically demanding it becomes. At the highest levels, it's on a par with tennis in its physical demands, and the best players may spend several hours a day on physical training. If you are interested in developing your skills even further, this step will help you with physical and mental conditioning.

WHY IS PHYSICAL CONDITIONING FOR TABLE TENNIS IMPORTANT?

If your opponent is in better physical condition, he or she has an advantage. A faster opponent gets to more balls and returns them more quickly. An opponent with more power is able to hit the ball past you easier than you can against your opponent. An opponent with more stamina plays better toward the end of a long match and is able to practice longer and harder. An opponent with more flexibility is able to adjust to different shots better than you will and will be less likely to sustain injuries. Is physical condition important to table tennis? YES!

Speed

To develop speed, jump rope (fast) and do multiple short sprints. Shadow practice your strokes and footwork. You can do this with or without a racket. Do it as fast as or faster than you would in a match. All top players shadow practice some. It not only builds up speed but allows you to practice movements without having to worry about the ball. (Perfect the move first and then learn to do it with the ball.)

Power

To develop power, lift weights or do calisthenics. But do high repetitions and low weight in whatever you do. You don't want to build big bulky muscles—you want fast and quick ones. Push-ups and sit-ups and similar exercises are ideal, as are nearly anything that builds up the legs and stomach. Few people realize how important the leg and stomach muscles are for table tennis. They're the support and pivot points for your body while you play. The forearm muscles of your playing arm are also of great importance. Keep in mind, however, that at the higher levels, you'll use just about every major muscle group, so you should develop them all.

Many top players use a weighted racket for training. It should weigh about three times what a normal racket weighs. Use it for shadow-stroking, but don't use it in a drill with a ball. You might hurt yourself, and it will throw off your timing when you go back to your normal racket.

Stamina

Stamina is important, both for those long 3 out of 5 matches after you've already played 10 matches in one day, and for practice. Who will improve faster, the player who can do a footwork drill at full speed for 10 minutes or the one who has to stop after 5? The importance of stamina is obvious. Long-distance running is the most common way to build this up, but an even better alternative is cycling, either on the road or on a stationary bike. This builds up stamina and leg strength. There are, of course, many other options. A game of full-court basketball played regularly (as the table tennis players at the Olympic Training Center do) is perfect, as are half a dozen other sports. Whoever said training had to be boring?

Flexibility

Flexibility is another aspect of fitness that's important to table tennis. The more flexible you are the easier it will be to make shots when you're slightly out of position and have to improvise. It also keeps you looser when you play, and perhaps most important, keeps you from getting injured. Before play, you should always stretch. (See "Warming Up For Success.") It's best to do some easy jogging first to get the muscles warmed up. Do this before you stretch. Make sure to cover each muscle group you'll use. After play, you might also want to stretch. You'll be looser then, and your muscles will stretch more. This will increase your general flexibility more than if you stretch when you are less loose. (Of course, if you run or play full-court basketball, afterward would also be a good time to stretch.)

WHY IS THE MENTAL GAME IMPORTANT?

Up until now, you've mostly learned the physical aspect of table tennis. You've learned a lot of strategy as well, which is one aspect of the mental game, but it goes far beyond that.

The mental game can be broken up into four parts:

- Tactical
- Mental rehearsal
- Arousal level
- Drive and desire

The tactical aspect has already been covered in Step 14, but not much has been said about the rest. Yet many consider these the most important parts. At the lower levels, the difference between two players is mostly physical, but at the higher levels, it's mostly mental.

There are many reasons why the mental game is significant. Mental rehearsal has been shown to help players improve. Players who cannot reach the proper arousal level (or get down to it if they're overaroused!) cannot be at their best. And those with the most drive and desire—well, they're the ones who end up with gold medals draped around their necks.

Let's look at the various aspects of the mental game.

Mental Rehearsal

Mental rehearsal is the act of imagining an event before doing it. For example, a bowler imagines throwing a strike, then tries to do it. A table tennis player can imagine that perfect smash on the sidelines over and over, and then when the shot comes up in the match, boom! The player is ready for it.

The mind often cannot tell the difference between what is actually happening and what is being imagined. So imagining a perfect shot is almost as good practice as doing that perfect shot! And no matter how uncoordinated you are, you can at least imagine yourself doing the shot.

Of course, mental rehearsal is not perfect. If you imagine yourself doing a 10-foot high jump, you still wouldn't be able to perform it. But if you mentally rehearse things that you can physically do, you may find yourself doing them better and

better. Imagining yourself making world champion-level shots may not make you the world champion, but it definitely will improve your game significantly.

There are two types of mental rehearsal. One is to simply imagine yourself doing something that is new for you, but that you've seen someone else do. The other is to imagine yourself doing something that you've already done well in the past, with the idea of doing it again.

When learning something new, or perfecting something you can already do, just close your eyes and imagine yourself doing it. You can do this anywhere, and you'll find yourself learning the new technique much more quickly.

When you're practicing or in a match, do the same. This time the object is to do something you can already do. For example, when serving, imagine the serve, or your follow-up shot. Picture it in your mind, then do it.

When doing mental rehearsal, you can either imagine yourself doing the perfect shot or actually remember a shot that you did in the past and use it as a model. Whenever you do something that you want to be able to do more often, remember what it felt like (using all the senses, if possible—especially sight, sound, and feel) and keep thinking about it. The next time that shot comes up, you'll probably do it just like you remembered.

Arousal Level

Different players have different ideal arousal levels. To play your best, you need to find the most appropriate arousal level for you and learn to reach that level during a match. In general, it is important to maintain a positive level of enthusiasm and energy to help direct your thoughts on the game. Once you have established what works for you, you will be able to concentrate better and ultimately play better.

Some players get nervous in a match. They're overly aroused and cannot play their best. This type of person needs to learn to calm down. Try breathing deeply; picture something relaxing (a field of grass or a blue sky are often used as examples). Try not to take the game so seriously!

Other players stay calm and collected throughout the match. In fact, they're so calm that they don't react well to shots, seeming almost lackadaisical. They want to play harder but can't. This type of player needs to get aroused, to get "psyched." The best way to do this is to talk to yourself. Tell yourself to fight, to play hard—whatever works! Be positive—say, "I can do this!" or "I'm going to attack!" As a last resort, you can increase your arousal level by telling yourself that the match is for the world championships.

Drive and Desire

Here I can't help you. The more drive and desire you have, the further you'll go. However, if you have too much of it, the game ceases to be fun. Eventually you burn out and quit. It would be better to relax and enjoy the game.

However much you want to put into the game is up to you. Regardless of physical talent (or lack of it), enough drive and desire will at least make you a pretty good player. With determination, practice, and patience you not only can enjoy the game, but learn to play at a high level.

Physical Drills

If you are really serious about improving your table tennis, or if you just want to see how the top players train, go through the following exercises. They are general exercises that will not only help you in table tennis, but in most other sports as well. They will also help you get into great physical shape!

1. 50-Yard Sprints (Speed and Stamina)

Sprint 50 yards as fast as you can, then jog or walk back briskly, and repeat. Always warm up the muscles and stretch before sprinting.

Success Goal = 5 to 8 sprints, three times a week

Your Score = (#) _____ sprints a week

2. Jumping Rope, Fast (Speed)

Make sure to use a ball-bearing rope or equivalent, if possible. If you aren't familiar with jumping rope, then begin slowly until you can do the entire 20 to 60 seconds without missing.

Success Goal = 20 to 60 seconds fast, three repetitions with a 30 to 60 second break between each repetition, 3 times a week (total of 180 to 540 seconds a week)

Your Score = (#) _____ seconds jumping rope fast a week

3. Weighted Racket (Strength)

With a weighted racket, practice all your shots away from the table. Shadow practice your shots; don't use a ball.

Success Goal = Shadow-stroke 100 forehands, 100 backhands, and 50 of each other stroke, three times a week

Your Score = (#) _____ strokes a week with weighted racket

4. Calisthenics (Strength and Stamina)

Push-ups, sit-ups, and step-ups are standard calisthenics, but feel free to add your own. When doing sit-ups, do them with slightly bent knees to take pressure off your back. These calisthenics are also good for stamina, especially muscle stamina (as opposed to cardiovascular stamina). To do a step-up, you step up onto a chair or other platform, then step down. Don't do this if you have bad knees.

Success Goal = 20 push-ups, 30 sit-ups, and 30 step-ups (or more), three times a week

Your Score =
  - (#) _____ sit-ups a week
  - (#) _____ push-ups a week
  - (#) _____ step-ups a week

5. Weight Training (Strength)

See a weight instructor to set up a good workout, or get a good manual, such as *Weight Training: Steps to Success*. Concentrate on the legs, waist, and arms, but strengthen the rest of the muscles as well. Nearly all muscles are used at some point in table tennis. It is strongly recommended that you have a weight instructor help set up your program and show you proper lifting techniques to avoid injuries.

Success Goal = Follow weight instructor's weekly program

Your Score = (#) _____ weeks following instructor's program

6. Running or Cycling (Stamina)

All top players run or cycle to build stamina in their legs. Without good stamina, you won't be able to move properly throughout an entire table tennis match. If you lack in agility, your opponent will have an advantage. Runners should use running shoes and avoid running on hard surfaces (which can lead to shin splints).

Success Goal =1 to 3 miles running or 3 to 10 miles cycling, three times a week

Your Score = (#) _____ stamina training drills a week

7. *Jumping Rope, Slowly (Stamina)*

This is probably the best stamina exercise for table tennis. It builds up the legs and arms, as well as cardiovascular fitness. Use a ball-bearing rope or equivalent and begin slowly. Your first few sessions of 1 to 5 minutes should be performed very slowly. Remember, the idea is to increase your aerobic stamina, not wear yourself out. As you become more accustomed to the exercise, gradually increase the duration that you jump. You can increase the speed if you want.

Success Goal = 1 to 5 minutes, three repetitions, three times a week, 9 to 45 minutes a week

Your Score = (#) _____ minutes jumping rope a week

8. *Flexibility*

See "Warming Up For Success" section, pages 7 to 9.

Success Goal = Follow warm-up routine before each time you play, at least three times a week

Your Score = (#) _____ stretching routines a week

Mental Drills

9. *Mental Rehearsal*

Think about each shot you want to learn or improve. Visualize doing each one successfully. Then go back to the step that explains the shot you wanted to improve. Choose a drill and do it. You are successful if you are able to do the shot that you have visualized.

Success Goal = Visualize yourself doing at least 10 different strokes, serves, or footwork movements and see how many you do correctly

Your Score =
- (#) _____ visualizations
- (#) _____ shots performed correctly

10. *Relaxation, Psyching*

Decide whether you're the type who needs to calm down when you play or needs to get psyched up. Before you play, concentrate on reaching the correct frame of mind. For example, if you are so excited that you begin to play sloppy shots, your arousal level is probably too high. Concentrate on your game and pay attention to technique. Also, try to relax when you play and enjoy yourself!

Success Goal = Be in the proper frame of mind during your next 10 practice sessions

Your Score = (#) _____ times in proper frame of mind during next 10 practice sessions

Playing in Tournaments

You've been practicing hard and have mastered much of what's in this book. You've beaten everyone on the block and knocked off some of the best players at your recreation center/club/basement. It's time to show the world. It's time to enter a tournament.

FINDING AND ENTERING TOURNAMENTS

First you have to find one to enter. If you've read the first section, you know about the USTTA. If you've joined, you should be getting a copy of its official magazine, *Table Tennis Today*. In it you'll find a tournament schedule for the entire country. If you don't have one, call or write USTTA headquarters. The address is in the "Table Tennis Today" section.

Some of the tournaments listed are small; some are large. You can tell by the prize money. Big ones have their prize money listed in the schedule, with the largest tournaments having the most. Smaller ones usually have prize money but the amount won't be listed. Some of the largest will have their entry blanks published in *Table Tennis Today*.

Find a tournament to your liking. If it's a good distance away you might have to fly or take a bus or train. If you need a hotel, one is usually listed on the entry blank. For your first tournament you might want to find a smaller one that isn't too far away. Or you might want to be dazzled by the best at one of the bigger ones. It's your choice.

There should be a tournament director listed for each tournament, with an address and phone number. Contact the director and he or she will send you an entry blank. If you go to that tournament, you'll be put on the mailing list; in the future you'll receive an entry blank automatically in the mail.

Look over the entry blank. Note the many events. It may look confusing but it's really quite simple. There should be a men's singles or open singles and a women's singles. There will probably be a few doubles events, such as open, men's, women's, or mixed. These should be quite clear. You'll find the best players playing in these events. There will probably also be some junior events.

The events you may not be familiar with will be the rating events that make up the majority of events. If there were only events such as open singles, all but the top players would be eliminated in the early rounds and beginners would be out in one match. That wouldn't be much fun.

Instead, all players who play in sanctioned USTTA tournaments are rated based on their results. This rating can range all the way from about 200 on up to the best in the U.S., which is usually somewhere around 2700. All players receive ratings after their first tournament, based on their results. The records of the games and matches (won or lost) as well as the point scores count for your initial rating, so fight for every point! After your initial rating, all that counts is whether you won or lost the match. The ratings are calculated by computer. The best players in the world often come to the U.S. and get ratings as well, some of which go over 2800. For comparison, a typical beginner takes a few months to reach 1000, if he or she practices.

If you're unrated and not sure which event to enter, contact the tournament director. You can enter as many events as you're eligible for unless the entry blank specifically says you can't. If you're in good shape and can afford it, enter a lot of events. Why not?

Another event that needs explaining is handicap singles. In it, you play one game to 51 points, spotting points according to your rating. In this event, anybody can beat anybody. If you're unrated, some tournament directors won't let you play. Others will watch you play in other events and estimate a rating.

Fill out the entry blank, write a check for the amount asked for and send it off. (Note that there will be a rating fee; it is mandatory. It is used to pay the rating chairman who works out your rating on a computer.) You're now as good as entered. It's time to get ready for the tournament.

PROPER REST AND NUTRITION FOR A TOURNAMENT

Everyone prepares for a tournament differently. Some rest the day before; others practice for hours. Do what's best for you. If you're in good shape, you should get at least some practice the day before. If not, you might want to rest. A tournament can be pretty tiring and you'll want to be well rested.

You should plan out your meals in advance. Most tournaments have food available but the menu isn't very good for an athletic event. Hot dogs are still standard, unfortunately. It's best to bring your own food or plan to eat out somewhere if you have transportation.

The night before a tournament it's best to eat foods high in carbohydrates. This will give you more energy the next day (it fills the muscles with muscle glycogen, which is what muscles use for energy) and is healthier as well. Of course, if you're playing strictly for fun, you shouldn't worry so much about your diet the day before.

On the morning of the tournament, eat early and well. You don't want to feel weak from hunger during the tournament. But again, eat mostly carbohydrates. Fat and protein stay in the stomach longer and will slow you down. (During digestion, blood is being used by the stomach. This reduces your energy level.)

Plan out your other meals. You don't want to eat a big (or medium) meal just before a match or you won't be at your best. If there are no long breaks, eat small snacks throughout the day. Fruit is good for this.

You'll need to drink lots of fluids during the tournament so as not to get dehydrated. Plain water is perfect but lightly sweetened drinks are also good. Sports drinks such as Gatorade are okay. Heavily sugared drinks will make you feel tired and should be avoided. (When your body finds extra sugar in the bloodstream, it pumps insulin into it. This removes both the extra sugar and the sugar that was there before. This leads to low sugar levels in the bloodstream and makes you tired.) Most tournaments have water fountains and soft drink machines. If you want something else, bring it with you.

WHAT TO DO AT THE TOURNAMENT SITE

Get to the tournament site early so you can practice. The later you get there, the more likely all the tables will be in use, and you'll have to wait for one to open up.

As soon as you arrive, register at the control desk. If it's your first tournament and you have questions, this is the time to ask.

Before warming up, do some easy jogging to get your muscles loose. (Many players jog before they eat breakfast, giving their muscles a head start.) Then stretch. (See "Warming Up For Success.") You won't be at your best unless your muscles are loose. Finish with some shadow-stroking.

Now warm up at the table. If all the tables are being used, you might have to double up. This means that four people warm up on one table. Two players hit crosscourt from the forehand side, the other two hit crosscourt from the backhand side. You can practice forehands or backhands from either side.

Practice all the shots you'll be using, including your footwork and serves. After the shots are feeling strong, play practice points or even a practice match. Don't do just rote drills until it's match time, or you won't be ready—play out some points.

If it's your first tournament, be ready for first-round jitters. If it's your 500th tournament, be ready for first-round jitters. In other words, they never go away. Get used to them. However, some handle them better than others. Just stay calm and remember that a million years from now the drawsheets will probably have been destroyed and nobody will remember what happened to you in the upcoming battle. Relax! Have fun!

Be ready when your name is called. You'll be given a match card, pencil, and ball and sent out to the table. You might even have an umpire for the match. Bring whatever you'll need for the match with you—towel, drink (for between games), maybe an extra racket, just in case. Shake hands with your opponent (both before and after the match, win or lose). The go to the table and beat the living daylights out of his or her game.

Rating Your Total Progress

Each step in this book covered specific items, with Success Goals given at the end. Below is a listing of these items. When doing the self-rating, be honest. Self-analytic skills are important to improvement.

You have to be able to honestly tell yourself what you're weak at—and what you do well. Then improve the weaknesses and make the strengths stronger!

PHYSICAL SKILLS	Very good	Good	Fair	Poor
Grip				
Ready stance				
Forehand drive				
Backhand drive				
Forehand smash				
Backhand smash				
Reading spin				
Racket angles				
Topspin serves				
Backspin serves				
Positioning				
Two-step footwork				
Beginning push				
Spin push				
Fast push				
Short push				
Forehand block				
Backhand block				
Forehand loop				
Backhand loop				
Crossovers				
Flip				
Stepping in				
Forehand chop				
Backhand chop				
Forehand lob				
Backhand lob				
Sidespin serves				
Fast serves				
Short serves				
Short serve receive				
Long serve receive				
Physical conditioning				

TACTICAL AND MENTAL SKILLS

	Very good	Good	Fair	Poor
Rallying tactics	_____	_____	_____	_____
Service tactics	_____	_____	_____	_____
Receive tactics	_____	_____	_____	_____
Mental imagery	_____	_____	_____	_____
Correct arousal level	_____	_____	_____	_____
Drive and desire	_____	_____	_____	_____

Your preceding responses should give you an indication for what you need to work on. They should also tell you what your strengths are—the skills and tactics that you may someday do better than anyone else, or at least better than your next opponent. As you improve at table tennis, you'll find that it's more a mental battle than a physical one. Accordingly, you need to hone your mental skills or you'll get left behind by the competition. Work on all of these skills in order to gain future success and enjoyment!

American grip—*See* **Seemiller grip.**

antispin—An inverted rubber sheet that's very slick, so spin doesn't take on it. It usually has a dead sponge underneath. It's mostly used for defensive shots. Also known as *anti*.

backhand—A shot done with the racket to the left of the left elbow for a right-hander, the reverse for a left-hander.

backspin—A type of spin used mostly on defensive shots. When you chop the ball, you produce backspin. The bottom of the ball will move away from you. This is also called **chop** or **underspin**.

blade— The racket, usually without covering.

block—A quick, off the bounce return of an aggressive drive done by holding the racket in the ball's path.

blocker— A style of play where blocking is the primary shot.

chop—A defensive return of a drive with backspin, usually done from well away from the table (see **backspin**).

chop block—A block where the racket is chopped down at contact to create backspin.

chopper—A style of play where chopping is the primary shot.

closed racket—Racket position in which the hitting surface is aimed downward, with the top edge leaning away from you.

counterdrive—A drive made against a drive. Some players specialize in counterdriving.

counterloop—To loop a loop (see **loop**).

countersmash—To smash a smash (see **smash**).

crosscourt—A ball that is hit diagonally from corner to corner.

crossover—A style of footwork for covering the wide forehand.

dead—A ball with no spin.

deep—1. A ball that bounces on the opponent's side of the table very close to the endline. 2. A serve or push that would not bounce twice on the opponent's side of the table (if given the chance).

default—Being disqualified from a match for any reason.

double bounce—A ball that hits the same side of the table twice. The person on that side loses the point.

down the line—A ball that is hit along one side of the table, parallel to the sidelines.

drop shot—Putting the ball so short that the opponent has trouble reaching it. Done when the opponent is away from the table.

expedite rule—If a game has continued for 15 minutes without the game ending, the expedite rule takes effect.

A point is awarded to the receiver who returns 13 consecutive shots after expedite has been called. Players alternate serves after expedite has been called.

flat—A ball that has no spin, usually traveling fast. The ball hits the racket straight on, at a perpendicular angle.

flip—An aggressive topspin return of a ball that lands near the net (a short ball).

footwork—How a person moves to make a shot.

forehand—Any shot done with the racket to the right of the elbow for a right-hander, to the left for a left-hander.

free hand—The hand not holding the racket.

handicap events—A tournament event where points are spotted to make the match even.

hard rubber—A type of racket covering with pips-out rubber but no sponge underneath. It was the most common covering for many years until the development of sponge rubber but is now rarely used.

high toss serve—A serve where the ball is thrown high into the air. This increases both spin and deception.

hitter—A style of play where hitting is the primary shot.

inverted sponge—The most common racket covering. It consists of a sheet of pimpled rubber on top of a layer of sponge. The pips point inward, toward the sponge, so the surface is smooth. This is the opposite of pips-out sponge, where the pips point outward, away from the sponge.

ITTF—International Table Tennis Federation. The governing body for world table tennis.

junk player—A player who uses an unusual racket covering, usually long pips or antispin.

kill shot—*See* **smash.**

let—If play is interrupted for any reason during a rally, a let is called and the point does not count. *See* "The Rules" in the "Table Tennis Today" section.

let serve—The most common type of let when a serve nicks the net. As with other lets, the serve is taken over again.

loaded—A ball with a great deal of spin.

lob—A high defensive return of a smash. Usually done with topspin or sidespin.

long—*See* **deep.**

long pips—A type of pips-out rubber where the pips are long and thin and bend on contact with the ball. It returns the ball with whatever spin was on it at contact and is very difficult to play against if you aren't used to it.

loop—A heavy topspin shot, usually considered the most important shot in the game. Many players either specialize in looping or in handling the loop.

looper—A style of play where the primary shot is the loop.

match—A two out of three or three out of five games contest.

open racket—Racket position in which the hitting surface is aimed upward, with the top edge leaning toward you.

penholder—A type of grip used mostly by Asians. It gives the best possible forehand but the most awkward backhand of the conventional grips.

pips—The small conical bits of rubber that cover a sheet of table tennis rubber.

pips-out—A type of racket covering. It consists of a sheet of pips-out rubber on top of a layer of sponge. The pips point outward, the opposite of inverted.

playing surface—The top of the table, including the edges.

push—A backspin return of backspin. Usually defensive.

put-away shot—*See* **smash**.

racket—What you hit the ball with. The blade plus covering.

racket hand—The hand that holds the racket.

rally—The hitting of the ball back and forth, commencing with the serve and ending when a point is won.

rating—A number that is assigned to all tournament players after their first tournament. The better the player, the higher the rating. The range is from about 200 to about 2900.

rating events—A tournament event that requires players to be rated under a specified amount.

receive—The return of a serve.

rubber—The racket covering. Sometimes refers only to the rubber on top of a sponge base.

rubber cleaner—Used to keep the surface of inverted rubber clean.

sandwich rubber—A sponge base covered by a sheet of rubber with pips that point either in or out. If pointed in, it is inverted sponge. If pointed out, it is pips-out sponge.

Seemiller grip—A grip that is often used in the United States, named after five-time U.S. National Champion Dan Seemiller, who developed it. Many coaches consider it an inferior grip and, outside the U.S. it is almost unheard of. Also known as the American grip.

serve—The first shot, done by the server. It begins with the ball being tossed from the palm of the hand and struck by the racket.

shakehands grip—The most popular grip. It gives the best balance of forehand and backhand.

short—A ball that would bounce twice on the opponent's side of the table if given the chance.

sidespin—A type of spin most effective on serves. When you use sidespin, the ball spins like a record on a record player.

smash—Ball is hit with enough speed so opponent cannot make a return. Also called a kill shot or a put-away shot.

smother kill—To smash right off the bounce. Usually done against a lob.

speed glue—A type of glue that can be put under a sheet of table tennis sponge to make it faster and spinnier.

spin—The rotation of the ball.

sponge—The bouncy rubber material used in sandwich covering under a sheet of rubber with pips. It revolutionized the game and ended the hard rubber age in the 1950s.

stroke—Any shot used in the game, including the serve.

topspin—A type of spin used on most aggressive shots, with an extreme amount being used in the loop shot. When you topspin the ball, the top of the ball moves away from you.

two-step footwork—The most popular style of footwork where the player starts with a short step with the foot on the side he or she is moving to. Then, the other foot follows as both feet move together.

umpire—The official who keeps score and enforces rules during a match.

underspin—*See* **backspin**.

USTTA—United States Table Tennis Association. The governing body for table tennis in the United States.

volley—To hit the ball before it bounces on your side of the table, which results in an immediate loss of the point for you.

About the Author

Larry Hodges is a past vice president for the United States Table Tennis Association (USTTA). He is also director and a coach at the National Table Tennis Center in Gaithersburg, Maryland. As a certified National Coach, Larry has worked with the best players in the country. He managed and coached at the Olympic Training Center in Colorado Springs from 1985 to 1989, and he was the U.S. Junior Coach at the U.S. Open Table Tennis Championships for 4 years. Larry has taught table tennis classes in colleges, recreation centers, clinics, and clubs all over the United States.

Larry was the editor of the USTTA publication *Table Tennis Today* from 1991 to 1995 and has also served as editor for *Table Tennis Coaches Quarterly*, another USTTA publication. He recently started his own magazine, *Table Tennis World*. He is also the author of the book *Instructors Guide to Table Tennis* and more than 300 articles on table tennis. Larry has been playing serious table tennis since 1976. He has been ranked among the top 30 players in the United States and has won state championships in North Carolina, Maryland, and Colorado. He is also a former National Collegiate Doubles Champion. When he's not coaching, playing, or writing about table tennis, Larry enjoys reading and writing science fiction, playing tennis and basketball, and tutoring kids in math and English.